Attention and Hyperactivity

a revision of
The Hyperactive Child

Second Edition

Ronald J. Friedman, Ph.D.
and
Guy T. Doyal, Ph.D.

IPP

The Interstate
Printers & Publishers, Inc.
Danville, Illinois

About the Authors

Dr. Ronald J. Friedman and Dr. Guy T. Doyal are child psychologists. In addition to their extensive clinical experience, they are both university professors involved in the training of psychologists and physicians.

Cover design by Mark A. Doyal

ATTENTION DEFICIT DISORDER AND HYPERAC-TIVITY, Second Edition. Copyright © 1987 by The Interstate Printers & Publishers, Inc. All rights reserved. First edition published under the title *The Hyperactive Child*, 1982. Printed in the United States of America. No part of this publication may be reproduced, stored in a retrieval system, or transmitted, in any form or by any means, electronic, mechanical, photocopying, recording or otherwise, without the prior written permission of the publisher.

Library of Congress Catalog Card No. 87-80913

3
4 5 6
7 8 9

ISBN 0-8134-2760-6

To Our Patients

Acknowledgments

We would like to express our appreciation to a number of people with whom we discussed the concept of this book and to several who read drafts as the manuscript developed and offered valuable advice and criticism. Psychologists Michael Merz and Michael McMillan provided us with considerable help. Linda Hryhorczuk, M.D., gave us the benefit of her considerable experience with hyperactive children in her critique of the manuscript. Other professionals and parents who read the first edition and offered comments and advice were immensely helpful, reminding us that our efforts had value only to the extent that we offered something useful to our patients and their families.

Contents

Introduction

This book has developed from our professional experience with a large number of children with Attention Deficit Disorder and hyperactivity. Over the years we have come to understand how much frustration and anguish is experienced both by hyperactive children and by those who live with, teach, or associate with them. Again and again we have been impressed with the sincerity of parents who desperately want to help their child and their family adjust to this disorder but are repeatedly frustrated in their efforts by the chronic nature of Attention Deficit Disorder.

We have often been moved by the sorrow we see in the faces of hyperactive children who, unable to control their behavior and bewildered by their inability to please their parents, teachers, and peers, stand frightened and angry over circumstances that they cannot deal with by themselves. At other times, we have observed in many families remarkable gains with all members of the family getting along harmoniously for a time. Then, although things go well for a while, the family experiences further troubles when a child reaches a different age and has different expectations and experiences thrust upon him or encounters new sources of stress as he matures and widens his experiences. These plateaus, peaks, and valleys cause a distressing emotional rollercoaster ride for everyone.

Although Attention Deficit Disorder and hyperactivity are among the most common behavioral problems in children, we have often been alarmed by the amount of misinformation and half-truths people labor under in trying to deal with their problem. Medical and psychological research has produced vast amounts of new information in the field, but this information is generally not readily available to parents and educators. In this book we have combined the most current medical and psychological research findings with our clinical experience with nearly a thousand children with Attention Deficit Disorder and their families with whom we have worked over the years. We have presented this information in this book in a way we hope will be useful to you as you care for your child with ADD. We suggest that you share this book with your child's teacher.

1 What Is Attention Deficit Disorder?

Attention Deficit Disorder (ADD) is a syndrome, a cluster of symptoms which include short attention span, difficulty concentrating, poor impulse control, distractibility, moods that change quickly, and in some cases, hyperactivity. Children who are overactive, impulsive, or highly distractible are often more difficult to manage than their less-active peers. As a result, they are more likely to develop behavior problems.

Attention Deficit Disorder is a relatively new term. Until about 10 years ago children who had one or more of the symptoms of ADD were often diagnosed as hyperactive. The disorder was originally labeled "Hyperactive Child Syndrome" because the overactivity of the child seemed to be the most important symptom. In recent years we have learned that activity level is a less important cause of behavioral and learning problems than is a short attention span—hence the change in the name from "Hyperactive Child Syndrome" to "Attention Deficit Disorder." Many children have all the other symptoms of ADD, but are not hyperactive. Throughout this book we will refer to children with Attention Deficit Disorder with Hyperactivity or Attention Deficit Disorder without Hyperactivity. (See "Revised Terminology and Diagnostic Criteria" in the Appendix.)

Along with overactivity, difficulty paying attention, and problems with impulsivity and moodiness, children with ADD also frequently have learning disabilities. Behavior problems often arise because parents, teachers, and other students find the child's overactivity or impulsivity troublesome. But many behavioral and family difficulties also result from the frustration, anger, and misunderstanding which are so frequently associated with the symptoms.

Experts in child behavior counsel parents to be firm and consistent in the way in which they manage all their children. This is excellent advice. But what of the child with ADD who is inconsistent himself? His behavior may appear to be unpredictable and even so unresponsive to a parent's attempts to control it that parents find it impossible to be consistent. As a consequence, in our clinic we frequently hear parents say, "We've tried everything. Some techniques of discipline seem to work for a while, but then they stop working, and now we don't know what to do. He seems to fight everything."

The Purpose of This Book

Our concern about management of children with ADD is not only that we want to make life more pleasant now while the children are young, but also that we are concerned about their later adjustment to school, work, and marriage. In this book we will offer practical guidelines for you to use in managing your child with Attention Deficit Disorder with or without Hyperactivity. The past 20 years have yielded a considerable body of psychological and medical research that is a rich source of information for those looking for guidance about how to manage such children. We have combined our own clinical experience with the information available from current medical and psychological research in order to provide the information contained in this book.

We will begin with a brief discussion of definitions and statistics. We don't want to burden you with an unnecessary amount of technical information or statistics, but some background is necessary, especially because the day-to-day behavior of children with ADD can be so puzzling and misleading. We often hear parents and teachers say:

"He just doesn't seem to care."

"He has the wrong attitude."

"She has to have it her way or not at all."

"If only he'd stop to think before he does something."

Each of these comments reflects one or more of the symptoms of the ADD syndrome. So the first place to start is with a clear understanding of the behaviors and personality characteristics under discussion. We will follow the material on definition and statistics with a careful review of medical, psychological, and educational management programs for youngsters with Attention Deficit Disorder.

Definition

The diagnostic criteria for Attention Deficit Disorder (ADD) with Hyperactivity have been established by the American Psychiatric Association. Such a child is inattentive, impulsive, and hyperactive. The symptoms are often worse in situations where the child must work on his own, such as in the classroom. The symptoms are not always present. Following are the criteria that define Attention Deficit Disorder with Hyperactivity:

A. Inattention—at least three of the following:
1. Often fails to finish things he or she starts
2. Often doesn't seem to listen
3. Is easily distracted

4. Has difficulty concentrating on schoolwork or other tasks requiring sustained attention
5. Has difficulty sticking to a play activity
B. Impulsivity—at least three of the following:
1. Often acts before thinking
2. Shifts excessively from one activity to another
3. Has difficulty organizing work
4. Needs a lot of supervision
5. Frequently calls out in class
6. Has difficulty awaiting turn in games or group situations
C. Hyperactivity—at least two of the following:
1. Runs about or climbs on things excessively
2. Has difficulty sitting still or fidgets excessively
3. Has difficulty staying seated
4. Moves about excessively during sleep
5. Is always "on the go" or acts as if "driven by a motor"
D. Problems begin before the age of 7 years.
E. Problems last at least 6 months.

The definition of Attention Deficit Disorder without Hyperactivity includes all these features except those listed under Section C, Hyperactivity. In many cases attention problems and impulsivity are milder when there is no hyperactivity.

Many children with ADD are also emotionally labile—their moods change abruptly. Parents often comment on how quickly their child's mood changes, not just from good to bad, but back to good again. So, in addition to the behavioral difficulties, children with ADD often seem more sensitive and easily upset. In some households this creates a constant level of tension as all family members go about their business ever mindful that there could be an emotional outburst at any moment.

The number of children who have Attention Deficit Disorder is difficult to determine, partly because different definitions have been used in the past to decide who has the disorder. Remember, until recently the main emphasis was on hyperactivity, so most children with Attention Deficit Disorder without Hyperactivity may not have been diagnosed properly and consequently not represented in the statistics. In general it is agreed that the disorder is common and that, in the United States, it probably occurs in about 3 percent of all children. Attention Deficit Disorder, either with or without hyperactivity, is six to eight times more common in boys than in girls, and although it is not inherited directly, the disorder does seem to be more common in some families than others. Because of the preponderance of males with ADD, most examples in this book will be boys. Nonetheless there are many girls with the disorder, and any example of male behavior used for illustration can be applied equally to females.

Secondary Symptoms

The life of a child with Attention Deficit Disorder is not easy. By the time a youngster with ADD is five years old and begins school, he probably has been criticized, corrected, and even rejected far more than an average child his age. When he begins school, the problems follow him there. Teachers may be critical of his inability to sit still and learn a lesson. In many instances, the youngster with ADD learns he is not progressing as fast as his classmates, and his self-esteem suffers.

Realizing that he has already been criticized more often than other children, knowing that disaster seems to follow him (more lamps break when he is in the room, more milk is spilled when he is at the table, more furniture is destroyed—and faster—when he is on the scene, and more children seem to wind up pushed down, poked, scratched, or bitten when he is in the group), the frustrations and failures of school don't come as a surprise. Often they serve to confirm for the child with Attention Deficit Disorder that he is bad, or stupid, or unacceptable in some other way. Individual children handle this in different ways, but it is common for them to become obstinate, occasionally negative, and often bossy or bullying. They may show low frustration tolerance and frequent outbursts because life is harder for them and more difficult for them to understand. Self-esteem suffers, and after a while it seems as if they don't respond to parents' efforts at discipline.

Consider for a moment how perplexing this must be to the five- or six-year-old child with Attention Deficit Disorder. Remember your own confusion and frustration and even anger as you tried to understand why your child was so difficult to manage and why he persisted in doing things that only seemed to lead to trouble. This comment from one mother conveys the feelings well. "He just pushes and pushes you until you want to . . . well, I hate to say it, but sometimes I just don't think I can stand it any longer." Well, if from your adult point of view you have been frustrated, confused, and angry, imagine what it must be like for your child. He hears from parents, teachers, brothers and sisters, and neighbor children a constant chorus reminding him that he is doing things wrong and is upsetting them, but he is unable to step back and understand and then control his own behavior in a way that enables him to satisfy other people and make them happy with his behavior.

Considering it from this point of view, it isn't surprising that many youngsters with Attention Deficit Disorder develop a second level of emotional and behavioral problems that can be traced back partly to the symptoms associated with their Attention Deficit Disorder, but also are a

4

result of the difficult and unpleasant experiences such youngsters encounter. Failure to understand how these two levels of problems go together is a cause of some of the difficulties and misunderstandings that parents and teachers have when trying to deal with children with ADD.

Effect on Parents and Families

Children with Attention Deficit Disorder often have a devastating effect on their families. Besides the obvious fact that it is difficult to raise a child who is more active, is into more things, and needs more supervision, there are other subtle ways in which children with ADD disrupt the quality of life. Mothers usually have the day-to-day responsibility for care, particularly when children are young. As a consequence, it is the mother who feels the greatest burden and the greatest frustration when there are problems. In the early years before the youngster's Attention Deficit Disorder is properly diagnosed, this frustration may result in conflict between husband and wife. Many fathers, because their tolerance for certain kinds of aggressive behavior is greater and because they don't see it on a constant basis as the child's mother does, think their son is nothing more than an active, normal boy.

It is common to have other family members say the same thing and subtly, if not directly, imply that the only reason the child is more difficult to manage is because of some inadequacy or failing on the part of the mother. Now the mother has three problems to deal with: an overactive child; frustration and anger because of the failure of other people, particularly her husband, to understand and to help; and finally, the beginnings of doubt about her own adequacy as a mother. It is a short step from this point to begin to wonder what she did wrong. She may begin to doubt her common sense and lose faith in her own judgment. Feeling terribly guilty is a natural result.

This combination of unpleasant feelings and attitudes often creates marital problems. The wife comes to feel increasingly misunderstood and overwhelmed with the responsibility of her child. The husband becomes angry with his wife because it seems that he can manage his child so much better than she can. It must be her fault, he concludes. And, because he is usually firmer, has a deeper voice, and has less contact with the child, it is not uncommon to see a child respond more quickly and consistently to his father's directions. A less dramatic version of this same pattern occurs in almost all families.

It would be an error to conclude that this proves the mother is the cause of the problem. It quickly becomes clear when a father spends a long time with his child that many of the same frustrating patterns become established as with the mother. With the increased strain in the marriage and the father's dissatisfaction with the way his wife and children are behaving, many fathers tend to pull back. For some this may mean finding excuses to come home for supper a bit later, but even in those cases where fathers don't go this far, they may subtly withdraw and cut down on the amount of time they spend with their wife or child. This may be illustrated by the father who watches TV, shutting out all of what is going on around him, reads a book, retires to a basement workshop, or escapes into a heavy work schedule. The effect is to drive a deeper wedge between husband and wife, weaken further the relationship of father and child, and finally, contribute greatly to feelings on the part of both parents that they are fighting a battle against a mysterious enemy they cannot quite understand or identify.

It is at this point that families often appear in doctors' offices voicing their concern about what is going on with their child, bewildered about the reasons for the difficulty.

What Causes Attention Deficit Disorder?

There are many unanswered questions about the origin, or etiology, of ADD, but research has given us some useful information. Children are probably born with Attention Deficit Disorder, although in many cases, when reconstructing with parents the child's early development, it is clear that symptoms may not be present from birth. While one mother may claim that her hyperactive youngster was more active even during her pregnancy, another may report that her child enjoyed unremarkable development until two or even three years of age, at which time the symptoms appeared. Nonetheless, appearance of symptoms when a child is two or three years old should not be taken to indicate that the disorder had not been present prior to this. Whatever the physical basis for the disorder might be, it is most likely that it existed from the beginning of the child's life, and it is only the symptoms that have been delayed in making their appearance.

Attention Deficit Disorder is not directly inherited, but there is a tendency for the problem to run in families, and there does seem to be some association with other problems of impulse control. For example, in one study 59 hyperactive children were compared to 41 children who were not hyperactive. The researchers found that 12 parents of the 59 hyperactive youngsters were retrospectively diagnosed as hyperactive, based on descriptions of behavior and old school records. However, only two parents of non-hyperactive children were regarded as possibly hyperactive. Statistics such as these make clear that hyperactivity is not directly inherited, but there is a greater incidence of hyperactivity in some families.

The fact that there is a tendency for Attention Deficit Disorder to run in families suggests that there might be a genetic or biological basis for the problem, at least to some extent and in some cases. Children can learn some habits that mimic the symptoms of Attention Deficit Disorder with Hyperactivity, although an experienced professional can usually distinguish between what might be regarded as a learned pattern of behavior and true Attention Deficit Disorder. Considering the state of our knowledge at present, Attention Deficit Disorder should best be regarded as having a physical basis, although neither the cause nor the precise mechanism which causes the symptoms is understood.

How Is Attention Deficit Disorder Diagnosed?

Obstacles to Early Diagnosis

One major problem in diagnosing Attention Deficit Disorder is that parents and especially teachers, who are in the best position to observe the symptoms when a child is young, do not think of ADD readily. We must know what we are looking for. We must be alert to the day-to-day ordinary behaviors that are symptoms of ADD if we hope to diagnose it as early as possible. We have to have what is called a "high index of suspicion" for a particular problem or diagnosis to have it pop into our minds when we see certain behavior patterns.

There is a saying among physicians, "When you hear hoofbeats you don't think of zebras." This odd expression is intended to remind doctors not only to keep in mind, when they hear or see any sign or symptom, the most obvious or most likely causes, but also to consider every possible cause, even those less likely to be involved. Only by considering every possible cause of the symptom or group of symptoms is the physician going to be sure to make a proper diagnosis.

By no means is ADD a rare phenomenon, but it would do a lot of good if everyone kept in mind a similar saying. As we will illustrate throughout the book, many symptoms of learning and behavior problems can be misleading. If a medical and psychological evaluation of a child is not sufficiently thorough, or if it is done by someone unaware of certain commonly occurring physical and psychological disorders, then it is likely that some children will be diagnosed incorrectly. The "zebra's hoofbeats" most often ignored or misunderstood by educators are the symptoms of Attention Deficit Disorder. You already know the technical definition of ADD, but what sorts of behavior do we see in the course of a normal day?

Short attention span, distractibility, and problems with impulse control have a direct effect on a child's behavior in the classroom and on his acquisition of academic skills. For example, it is common to see a child in first or second grade who does not complete his work. Careful observation reveals that the child can and will do the work if someone stands over him and supervises on a one-to-one basis. Because a child works well one-to-one and clearly can learn, it is easy to conclude that the child can do it if he wants to. This seemingly innocent observation and conclusion can be the first step toward a destructive and hurtful process that causes considerable harm for the child and his family.

While there are many possible explanations for why a child may not complete his schoolwork, it is rarely recognized by educators that ADD is one of the most common. Too often such a youngster is viewed as either unmotivated or immature. He may be thought to lack a good attitude toward school. It is not uncommon to hear such behavior described as "attention seeking," based on the fact that the child does so well when you give him attention. This is a serious misunderstanding of the circumstances in most cases. The reason a child does well when he is given attention is because the parent and/or the teacher organize things for the child and use their own longer attention span and ability to focus on materials to help keep the child oriented to the task.

Failure to complete any schoolwork, then, is one of the zebra's hoofbeats. It should sound an alarm. It should raise your index of suspicion. It should cause you to ask whether the child possibly has Attention Deficit Disorder.

Similarly, the child with "motor mouth" in kindergarten or the youngster who always pushes and gets in trouble when standing in line may be presenting signs of Attention Deficit Disorder. A child who does not seem able to wait his turn and constantly blurts out answers in class without raising his hand first may be demonstrating symptoms of poor impulse control.

These are all the zebra's hoofbeats. These are all the symptoms or behavior that should alert parents and teachers to the possible presence of ADD. Such behaviors, if misunderstood or dismissed as immaturity, may be the foundation for later learning and psychological problems.

Even though it may be obvious, we want to caution the reader in one important regard. This is a book about Attention Deficit Disorder and hyperactivity. There are other problems that also produce the behavior we have described here. Not every child who fails to complete an assignment or talks out of turn has Attention Deficit Disorder. Our concern, however, arises from the fact that failure to consider Attention Deficit Disorder as one possible cause of these behaviors leads to many cases of ADD going undiagnosed. A diagnosis of Attention Deficit Disorder can only be made by a physician or psychologist who specializes in work with children and is knowledgeable about all of the possible causes of the behavior that gives us concern.

The criteria used for deciding whether a child has Attention Deficit Disorder with or without Hyperactivity have been described above. Let us consider how they are applied in actual practice. There are no specific tests for Attention Deficit Disorder or for hyperactivity. There are several rating scales or check lists that help the professional organize his or her observations or help parents and teachers describe the behavior of children, but these tests do not tell directly whether a child is hyperactive or has Attention Deficit Disorder. For example, we can rate a child's squirminess as he sits at the dinner table or in the classroom. Many hyperactive youngsters are quite fidgety. But so are children with other sorts of problems. One of the most common reasons for being overactive is anxiety. Nervous children may display symptoms identical to those of a child with ADD. They may move about restlessly or, because their mind is on some troubling matter at home or with friends, not pay attention to the lesson in school. So we see it is not possible to make a diagnosis of Attention Deficit Disorder or hyperactivity only on the basis of even a very careful description of behavior.

In a similar fashion, there is no medical test such as a blood test or other medical procedure that allows us to make this diagnosis with certainty. Rather, the physician and and psychologist make use of several sources of information that can be put together with their professional experience to yield a decision about whether your child has Attention Deficit Disorder.

History

The child's past history is the most important source of information. Although it amuses many observers, mothers of hyperactive youngsters often say that they knew that their child was more active while they were still carrying him. "I think my ribs were bruised from the inside from the sixth month on," one mother said with a hint of a smile. The history of most children with Attention Deficit Disorder is not that clear. But usually careful questioning by a professional and equally careful thought and reconstruction of a child's early years by the mother and father yield important information about activity level and early temperament patterns.

We try to determine whether the child was more squirmy as an infant, possibly more colicky, more irritable. A common feature in the early history of youngsters who are later determined to have Attention Deficit Disorder is the report that "he didn't adjust to new circumstances very well." For instance, when changes in feeding were instituted or attempts were made to change babysitters or sleep habits, the child found it more difficult than other children to get used to the new routines.

As a child gets older, it is important to give some thought to how well he is able to pay attention compared to other children. Did he sit quietly and listen to a story when he was three years old? How long could he sit and go through a picture book with his mother? Did he watch television? Did he ever watch a television program all the way through? There are long lists of such questions that you can probably develop yourself that would give you some idea about how impulsive, active, and attentive your children have been.

Inborn Temperament Characteristics

No two children are born with exactly the same behavioral characteristics. Just as there are both dramatic and subtle differences in the physical appearance of children, even those born to the same mother and father, there are comparable differences in temperament, personality characteristics, and behavioral style.

Any attempt to ascertain whether a child has Attention Deficit Disorder must include both a careful reconstruction of the child's early temperament pattern and also efforts to determine whether the problematic behavior reflects ADD, is the expression of temperament characteristics, or is a combination of both.

Parents and child-care professionals have long known that there were striking differences among young children, but a systematic approach to the study of newborn behavior and its contribution to child development began with the work of a pediatrician and two child psychiatrists, Alexander Thomas, Stella Chess, and Herbert Birch. Their research began in the late 1950's, and although the first reports were published a decade later, it was not until the past 10 years or so that pediatricians and psychologists began to apply the results of these studies in a systematic way to child care and parent counseling.

Child-care professionals are now able to identify nine inborn behavior patterns called *temperament characteristics,* based on meticulous observation and descriptions of child behavior, supplemented with research and clinical experience which was built on a foundation established by the pioneering research. These characteristics of temperament provide a good picture of the biological basis of a child's behavior.

The temperament of all children can be described and measured. The importance of this fact takes on special significance in the case of children with Attention Deficit Disorder and hyperactivity because we have one more tool to use when we make our observations and attempt to understand the significance of a child's behavior. With the understanding that arises from our knowledge about temperament, children's behavior makes more sense to parents and professionals. This deeper understanding also allows greater precision in parenting, teaching, and child management counseling.

1. *Activity level* refers to the tempo and frequency of movements. A very active child may run, kick, squirm, or crawl all over the house. A child with a low activity level usually doesn't kick and fuss, lies quietly in the bath, or in the morning is still lying in the same place where he fell asleep. These are extremes; most children fall somewhere in between.

2. *Rhythmicity* reflects the degree of regularity of biological functions such as sleeping and waking, and rest and activity, as well as food intake and elimination cycles.

3. *Approach or withdrawal* describes the initial reaction when a child encounters something new, such as food, toys, people, places, or procedures. Some parents describe children who cry when they see a stranger; their preponderant style is to withdraw. Other parents describe their children with comments such as "She always smiles at a stranger," or "If he sees a new toy, he goes straight for it." The last two are approach reactions.

4. *Adaptability* is related to approach or withdrawal, which refer to the initial response a child makes. Adaptability deals with the ease with which the initial pattern is changed. So, the child who spat out cereal when it was first fed to him, but later came to accept it with a little response, is considered adaptable, while the child who continues to reject food displays nonadaptive behavior.

5. Whether a behavior is positive or negative, it can appear with a high or low *intensity.* Every child has a dominant characteristic which determines the intensity of his behavior in all situations.

6. *Threshold of responsiveness* refers to the intensity of stimulation required to elicit a response from a child. Thresholds may differ for different sensory systems. A child can have a high threshold for visual stimulation, but a low auditory threshold. Some children appear to be very sensitive to any sort of stimulation, while others are best characterized by the statement one mother used to describe her child, "A bomb could go off in his room and he wouldn't bat an eye."

7. *Quality of mood* differentiates between a child whose mood is friendly and pleasant and the child who tends to behave in a generally unfriendly or unpleasant manner.

8. *Distractibility* indicates the ease with which behavior can be interrupted by noise or sounds that occur around the child or the distractions provided by the activity of other people.

9. The last temperament category reflects the child's *attention span and persistence.* Attention span refers to the length of time an activity is pursued; persistence relates to whether an activity is maintained despite distraction and other obstacles. A child can be both highly distractible and highly persistent. Such a child would return to a task again and again, no matter how often he is distracted or diverted.

As might be expected, few children fall at the extremes. Also, if a child's behavior reflects problems at the extreme limits of only one or two categories, he will not be especially difficult to manage.

The "Difficult Child." There is, however, a group of children whose behavioral style is marked by irregularity, nonadaptability, withdrawal, and predominantly negative moods of high intensity. Not surprisingly, research workers and clinicians chose to call such children "difficult." As infants, difficult children often wake at unpredictable intervals and seem to require less sleep than the average child of the same age. Since such children do not develop regular sleep cycles as quickly as others, these infants' parents are awakened several times a night and, no matter what technique they might try, they find it impossible to get their child to sleep at night. Similar unpredictability can often be found in the way hunger is expressed. This may be true of elimination cycles as well, and toilet training procedures seem much more difficult. Such children are often described as fretting when bathed for the first time, crying whenever a new food is introduced, fussing whenever a new person enters the room. Leaving the house may result in crying, protesting, and clinging, and the same behavior may occur when the family returns home. The predominance of high-intensity negative mood is shown by relatively more crying than laughing and more fussing than expressions of pleasure.

Most parents will never have children with this clear-cut difficult-child temperament pattern; however, many children will display some of these features. Not all children with difficult temperaments develop serious behavioral or psychological problems. Nonetheless, such children are more difficult to rear, and much depends on the particular combination of child personality characteristics and parent temperament patterns. The history of each child must be carefully evaluated to determine whether a difficult temperament is the primary problem or if it co-exists with Attention Deficit Disorder.

Tests

The evaluation of a child suspected of having Attention Deficit Disorder often includes a battery of psychological and educational tests. While the tests do not lead directly to the diagnosis, they are useful in clarifying certain aspects of a child's behavior. Test scores also provide measurements to be used later for comparison to assess how effective treatment is.

Intelligence tests are an important part of the psychological evaluation. Usually these tests are used because a child with suspected ADD often has learning problems. We must determine if the learning problems reflect limited intellectual ability. In addition, the most commonly used intelligence test, the Wechsler Intelligence Scale for Children–Revised, consists of 10 different subtests, each of which gives the psychologist some specialized information. For example, there are several subtests that measure short-term memory and concentration. The fact that a child scores more poorly in these areas than in other portions of the test is additional information that can be used to decide whether a child has an attention problem.

Other commonly used tests of intelligence include the Stanford-Binet Intelligence Scale, the Bayley Test of Mental Development, the Peabody

Picture Vocabulary Test, and the Kaufman Assessment Battery for Children.

Educational tests are designed to measure a child's achievement in reading, spelling, arithmetic, and other academic areas. Educational tests allow the psychologist to determine the child's achievement level under the best circumstances. Classroom grades often reflect more information than just how much the child has learned. Study habits, incomplete papers, poor preparation for tests, or troublesome behavior in the classroom may all be reflected in a child's grades. Educational tests are necessary in order to determine just how much of a handicap the Attention Deficit Disorder might be and what areas are being affected.

Among the most commonly used educational tests are Wide Range Achievement Test, Woodcock-Johnson Psychoeducational Battery, Stanford Diagnostic Reading and Math Tests, Test of Written Expression, and Kaufman Test of Educational Achievement.

There are two types of *personality tests*. Objective personality tests have clear-cut questions and answers. The Personality Inventory for Children and Minnesota Multiphasic Personality Inventory are objective personality tests often used in the assessment of children and their families.

Projective personality tests are less clear-cut in what they require a person to do. The Sentence Completion Test, for example, presents the child or adult with a series of partially completed sentences and the person has to complete the phrase with any idea he chooses. In this case, although the first few words of the sentence are clear, the person can respond in a variety of ways. The psychologist analyzes the content and pattern of the sentences written.

The Rorschach Inkblot Test is another example of a projective test. Here it is not only the individual's answers which may come from a variety of thoughts or ideas, but even the nature of the test item itself, the inkblot, is ambiguous. Personality tests of this sort are helpful because they enable a psychologist to gain additional insight into a person's thoughts and feelings and also help determine whether other psychological factors are contributing to the problems in addition to, or instead of, Attention Deficit Disorder.

Other examples of projective personality tests include the Thematic Apperception Test (TAT) and Family Drawings.

A variety of *other specialized tests* may be included in the assessment of a child or an adult. Among the most common are those referred to as perceptual tests. The Bender Visual Motor Gestalt Test and the Beery Developmental Test of Visual Motor Integration are the most common. Related tests include the Visual Aural Digit Span Test and the Matching Familiar Figures Test.

Rating Scales

As so often happens, decisions about whether a child is hyperactive or has Attention Deficit Disorder are not difficult to make in extreme cases. Rather, it is when children are only moderately overactive or inattentive that we have difficulty determining whether this represents a true case of Attention Deficit Disorder or whether this is just a youngster whose motor runs a little bit faster than does that of an average child. Along with the careful history and test data we also want another piece of information—how is a child behaving right now? Parents and teachers provide valuable information in this regard. You can give a long-term, careful, historical point of view about your child, and a teacher is often in a valuable position to describe a child's current behavior compared to a large number of other children his age.

There are a number of rating scales that have been developed to organize this task for parents, teachers, and other professionals attempting to determine if certain behaviors are severe enough to be regarded as significant problems. Typically, the rating scales consist of anywhere from 10 to 30 short descriptions of behavior such as those listed below.

1. Fidgets and can't sit still   Always Sometimes Rarely Never
2. Speaks up or calls out in
   a disruptive manner   Always Sometimes Rarely Never
3. Finishes schoolwork   Always Sometimes Rarely Never
4. Follows directions well   Always Sometimes Rarely Never

It can be seen from this that the rating scale does not make a diagnosis. All it gives is a description of behavior, but it is a well-organized description. Along with the history and observations that doctors make in their examining rooms, this rating scale provides information about whether a child has, indeed, ADD and helps make the diagnosis. Standardized questionnaires and rating scales are especially useful in evaluating the symptoms of ADD because opinions about the severity or seriousness of behavior varies from observer to observer, possibly reflecting the observer's tolerance for certain behavior. Also, the child's behavior may be different from one day to the next, so the written questionnaire helps ensure that everyone is reporting on and making comparisons based on the same information. A list of well-known rating scales is included at the end of the book for further reference.

2 Medical Treatment and Management

In the following four chapters we will discuss a number of different ways to help children with Attention Deficit Disorder. Chapters 2, 3, and 4 deal with medical, psychological, and educational considerations. Chapter 5 stresses problem prevention.

With the current state of our knowledge, there are limits to what we can do to help children with Attention Deficit Disorder. As a result, the problem cannot be cured in the sense that we usually think of a cure— the absolute elimination of the disorder. Rather, we tend to think in terms of how best to control or manage these difficult and often destructive sorts of behavior. Fortunately, parents find that once they can sort behavior into these two categories, "something can be done" and "nothing can be done," this, itself, reduces some of the frustration. It also emphasizes to many parents that these behaviors are not their fault. Learning the difficult, but rewarding, lesson about how to live with the problem is one of the most important things that can be done.

Medication

The discussion that follows applies to Attention Deficit Disorder with or without Hyperactivity. Medication may be helpful for any single symptom or a combination of symptoms.

Three broad classes of drugs have been used with children with hyperactivity and ADD, stimulants, tranquilizers, and antidepressants. Many people are surprised that the stimulant medications are far more effective in aiding youngsters with ADD than are tranquilizers and other drugs that are generally used to calm people down. As in any medical matter, your child's physician should be your guide and source of information in using medicine to treat ADD. The discussion below is intended to familiarize you with some of the medicines that are used, as well as some of the issues involved in how to decide what medicine to use, what dosage to prescribe, and why the medicines work the way they do. But this discussion would be insufficient for anyone to use as a guide for managing a particular child, and it is important for you to realize that you may risk your child's safety if you try to alter any dose or type of medicine after reading this material without first discussing it thoroughly with your child's physician.

Tranquilizers

Some physicians have used tranquilizers to try to control overactivity and problems with impulse control, but generally with poor results. The most commonly used tranquilizer is thioridazene (Mellaril). Mellaril has been used mostly to control extreme agitation and organically based temper tantrums which, at times, have a major aggressive element. Minor tranquilizers, such as Valium and Librium, have been used, as have antihistamines, such as Benadryl. While there may be a use for tranquilizers in a very few, limited cases, for the most part they are less effective and less desirable than the stimulants for treating Attention Deficit Disorder and hyperactivity.

Stimulants

The most commonly used stimulant drugs are methylphenidate (Ritalin), dextro-amphetamine (Dexadrine), and magnesium pemoline (Cylert). The use of stimulant drugs such as these has its origin in the use of Benzedrine in the 1930's, so we can see physicians have had many years' experience using such types of medicine. Current estimates are that approximately 600,000 children in North America are being treated with stimulant medication.

Although the exact neurological mechanisms to account for why these stimulants help children with ADD are not completely clear, there are several theories based on recent research which have begun to shed light on the question. Stimulants appear to increase the amount or efficiency of chemical messengers in the central nervous system. At one time, it was thought that there was some problem in a child's central nervous system which caused him to react to stimulant drugs in the opposite way to which we would expect. Rather than becoming stimulated and more aroused when given a drug such as Ritalin, hyperactive children settled down. Now, we realize that this is not a paradoxical, or opposite, reaction at all. In fact, new findings have shown that children without ADD also concentrate better when given Dexadrine or Ritalin. In the past few years, we have gained a better understanding of how the nervous system works, and several hypotheses have been put forward to explain the way in which the stimulants work. While none of these hypotheses has been conclusively proven, the mechanism by which the beneficial effect occurs is probably something like this.

In order for any of us to pay attention and concentrate, we must be able to ignore many irrelevant things that are going on around us all the time. As you read these words you may be sitting in a noisy house. Perhaps there is a television set or phonograph playing in another part of the house. There may be background sound from a fan in your furnace or air conditioner. Cars may be passing in the street outside your home. Of course, if it is too noisy, if there are too many distractions, you cannot concentrate. But most people are able to filter out or ignore stimulation that is in the background, and this helps them concentrate on what they are doing.

Usually, we do not do this consciously; we do not make a decision to ignore each of these stimuli. Rather, our nervous system does it for us automatically. Children with Attention Deficit Disorder seem to be less efficient at doing this. They can, of course, concentrate to some extent. They can filter out some of this noise and activity in the background, but they do not do it as well as we would like. This is where the medicine becomes useful.

Why some children have this problem is unclear, but there are probably several different reasons. In some cases, genetic factors are prominent. Such difficulties may run in families. Birth problems such as insufficient oxygen at some point could contribute to Attention Deficit Disorder, as could certain infections. However, in most cases we do not know the cause. Nonetheless, we see the beneficial effect of medicine. The drug stimulates and improves the efficiency of the part of the brain that acts as the filtering mechanism to screen out these outside stimuli. It stimulates an inefficient system to work more efficiently. When the drug is working well, all it accomplishes is to make the child's nervous system work in a normal fashion.

Now, the complete theory is more complex than this, but it helps us understand how a drug such as Ritalin enables a child to pay attention better, control his impulses better, and become less distractible and less hyperactive. As you can see, the drug seems to work by normalizing the functioning of the child's nervous system, rather than by tranquilizing him or calming him down or, in any other way, interfering with the normal functioning of his body. This is the reason why stimulant drugs are preferred over tranquilizers or other medicines that have their effect by making a child drowsy or impairing the efficiency of his nervous system and body.

Antidepressants

One class of antidepressant drugs known as tricyclics has been used with some success to treat ADD. Tricyclics are usually used when stimulants have already been tried but either are not effective or produce too many side effects. The most commonly used tricyclic antidepressant is imipramine (Tofranil). Another frequently used drug in the same category is amitryptaline (Elavil).

The tricyclics are not as widely effective as stimulants, and it often takes a longer period of time to see the positive effect of the medication, sometimes as long as three to four weeks. Another factor that makes antidepressants a second choice in the treatment of ADD is that there are side effects to be concerned about. In some cases antidepressants have an effect on the heart. A doctor who chooses to prescribe an antidepressant for the treatment of ADD will do a series of routine studies, including an electrocardiogram (EKG) to monitor the patient's heart activity.

How the Doctor Decides What Drug to Use

There are no absolute guidelines to help a physician know which drug to prescribe. Approximately 75 percent of children with ADD respond positively to some extent to one of the stimulants. Among the children who do not respond to stimulants there are some, according to a recent research report, who do not absorb the drug from the digestive system in a way that provides behavioral change. Some children who respond well to Ritalin do not do well on Dexadrine or Cylert. The opposite is also true. Usually a physician prescribes the drug with which he has had the most experience and one he thinks, in his professional judgment, is best for the child. In some cases it is necessary to change the prescription and try a different medicine. This a safe procedure and, although it delays getting the child's behavior under control by a few weeks, there are no other negative effects associated with it.

Ritalin is the drug with which pediatricians, child psychiatrists, and pediatric neurologists are most familiar, so it is prescribed most often. The third medicine mentioned, Cylert, is the newest of the three. Ritalin and Dexadrine may be administered in several doses at roughly four-hour intervals throughout the day or in a single sustained-release, or spansule, form once in the morning. Only one form of Cylert is available, a long-acting dose taken in the morning.

The sustained-release, or longer-acting, medications have several advantages. They reduce the possibility of error and forgetting a noon-time dose if a child does not come home from school for lunch. It also saves the social embarrassment of being different from other students for older children, particularly teenagers, who are often self-conscious and embarrassed about having to go to the principal's or nurse's office for medicine at lunchtime. This is one of the most common reasons teenagers are sometimes difficult to manage with medicine, leading to a child finding ways to avoid the medicine, which then leads to conflict with parents and teachers. Long-acting medication such as Cylert and sustained-release Ritalin and Dexadrine offer a welcome opportunity to avoid this sort of embarrassment and conflict. Nonetheless, there are instances when divided doses throughout the day have a better therapeutic effect or are more desirable for other reasons.

Some children who respond well to divided doses of Ritalin may not have an equally positive response to the sustained-release form of the medication. Many children do not do as well on sustained-release Ritalin (Ritalin SR) as on divided doses. This is especially important to keep in mind if your child has been doing well for a period of time taking medicine in the morning and at lunchtime and, for convenience, your doctor switches to Ritalin SR. Be alert for changes in behavior. Keep in mind that if the quality of behavior or schoolwork deteriorates, this may reflect the lessened effectiveness of the medication.

Why some children respond well to divided doses of Ritalin and not to the sustained-release formula is unclear. There is some preliminary evidence to suggest that in some children Ritalin SR is not absorbed evenly throughout the day from the digestive system, and consequently the therapeutic level in the bloodstream varies more than with the divided doses.

The decision about whether to administer the medicine several times through the day or in a form that requires only a single administration in the morning is something that should be discussed with your child's doctor.

How Does the Doctor Decide on the Dose?

Just as choosing a drug is a matter of making an initial careful trial, so is deciding on a proper dose. Most physicians begin a child on a small dose of a stimulant and then wait to see what effect this has on behavior. If necessary, the medicine can be increased in small steps until the desired effect is obtained, or it becomes clear that the medicine is not helping, at which point it is discontinued and another drug is tried. The therapeutic effect may be evident within a few days with Ritalin or Dexadrine and may take longer with Cylert.

Research in the past few years has shown that it is no longer sufficient just to ask, what is the best dose of medication for a child? Rather, we must ask what is the best dose for this particular child and for what particular purpose? The dose of a stimulant necessary to bring a child's hyperactivity under control may not be the same dose required to provide the best control of the problem he has paying attention. To complicate this matter even more, a different dose may be required to gain maximum control of impulsivity, and still a different dose for the best effect on emotional changes.

Fortunately, for most people the doses necessary for different problem areas are roughly the same. For some children, they are identical. Nonetheless, for a number of children we have to compromise and make a decision about which aspect of the symptom pattern we are most concerned about. To get optimum control in one area we must recognize that we may have to sacrifice some control of other symptoms.

Even if it is impossible to obtain perfect control of all symptoms, understanding the way the medicine works on different symptoms helps us plan more effectively. For example, consider the child who has a short attention span and is hyperactive. Behavior modification techniques are more effective and easier to implement for hyperactivity than for short attention span. Under such circumstances, if we cannot get maximum effective control of both sets of symptoms with medication, our choice would be to regulate the medicine based on improvement in attention span and completion of schoolwork and use a behavior modification program for the symptoms reflecting overactivity, such as running or frequently getting out of the chair.

A full understanding of treatment with medicine helps make clear why it sometimes takes so long to arrive at a proper dosage for a child. Not only must we begin with a small dose and work up to the point where we get the therapeutic effect we want, but at that stage we still may have to make adjustments once we have determined more thoroughly how well the child is doing.

One further element to this discussion should be highlighted. Some behavior is easier to measure. For example, if a child is very active it is not too hard to see whether medicine slows him down. On the other hand, if a child has only a subtle disturbance in attention span that causes his learning to be inefficient, that may be harder for a teacher to assess. Progress in attainment of academic skills is not something that can be measured on a day-to-day basis. Consequently, for many physicians it has been the practice to titrate, or regulate, the dose of medicine based on the parents' and teachers' reports of the most observable behavior. That means that activity level or impulse control problems may have been used as a measure of effectiveness of the medicine. The fact that it may not be the optimal dose for learning is then neglected. So, using activity level to regulate the dose, after a period of time the child's behavior is under better control. If, however, the teacher finds that learning has not progressed at a commensurate rate, further adjustment in the child's medicine dose may be necessary, sacrificing some control in behavioral areas in order to attain better performance in achievement.

Use of Medication with Adolescents and Adults

It remains common practice among many physicians to routinely stop prescribing medication for children with ADD when they reach a certain age. While it is true that the need for medication should be reassessed at intervals, there is now a substantial amount of evidence that stimulants continue to be helpful, not only during the teenage years, but into adulthood as well.

The reason many practitioners discontinue medication when a child is 13 or 14 years old seems to be based on two mistaken notions. First, it has long been thought that children outgrow Attention Deficit Disorder when they reach the early stages of puberty. This erroneous conclusion is based on the observation that many children do, indeed, become less active at that time. If the psychologist or physician looks only at activity level without considering impulse control problems and attention span, the conclusion may be that the problem no longer exists.

The second reason for failure to continue using psychostimulants with teenagers and young adults is that, until the last few years, there had been no published reports in the adolescent or adult psychiatric journals that demonstrated that medication was helpful. That research has now been done, and the publication of several influential articles in *Pediatrics, Journal of Child Psychiatry,* and *The American Journal of Psychiatry* have made practitioners more aware of the value of medication with older individuals. Moreover, research by a team of doctors at the Children's Hospital of Montreal, Canada, led to the recent publication of the book *Hyperactive Children Grown Up.* The authors found that the symptoms of ADD continue to be a pervasive and chronic problem for adults.

Decisions to treat older adolescents and adults with medication should be based on the same criteria as for deciding to treat younger children. First, the diagnosis has to be made. Then, a determination must be made of the extent to which the symptoms of Attention Deficit Disorder interfere with the person's life. For many adults, medication will not be necessary. Simply understanding Attention Deficit Disorder in its adult form and recognizing how the symptoms affect day-to-day living, work, and family relationships is often immensely helpful in enabling the adult with ADD to accept his symptoms and compensate for them. In some cases medication is appropriate. For example, we have observed the benefits of Ritalin for adults who are going to school. Certain occupations require sustained attention, and often medication enables a person to work with greater efficiency.

We cannot overemphasize the value of making the diagnosis of ADD in an adult. In Chapter 4 we will have more to say about the special problems parents with ADD have in managing children with ADD. At this point, we only want to stress the importance of recognizing that ADD persists throughout life and that the symptoms that are so troublesome for children can be equally, if not more, troublesome for adults.

Other Points About Treatment with Medication

It is important that you administer your child's medicine according to the instructions of his physician. Many problems can be traced to poor habits in taking medicine, such as changes in dose frequency or size of dose without physician consultation. Your child's doctor might give you some discretion in adjusting the dose of medicine, taking into consideration your reports about your child's behavior as well as using his or her medical judgment about your child. Without that instruction, you should stick carefully to the prescribed schedule.

One reason this is so important is that stimulant drugs work differently from some other medicines with which people are most familiar, such as antibiotics which are prescribed for a short period of time and usually "cure" the child's illness. Stimulant drugs do not cure children with ADD, with or without Hyperactivity. Continued use of the medicine on a regular basis is necessary. Also, most parents are used to the idea that either you have an illness or you don't. That model of disease is not appropriate when considering Attention Deficit Disorder. The difficulty arises when, after a child has been symptom-free for a few weeks or a month, some parents get a little sloppy with the medicine. It is as if they say to themselves, "Well, I guess we finally have this under control," and then they forget a dose of the medicine and the behavior problems reappear.

There is another misunderstanding that is common. Keep in mind that children with Attention Deficit Disorder are far more normal than abnormal. As normal children, they have the usual moods and temperament changes that you might expect. Like everybody else, they have good days and bad days, happy days and sad days. There are days when they are irritated and cannot wait to get through the day, and there are days that they greet with enthusiasm and joy. Because your child has a fight on the playground similar to the fights he had before you began to treat him with medicine, is no reason to assume that the medicine is no longer working properly. Children have fights on the playground and get into other sorts of trouble for reasons that have absolutely nothing to do with hyperactivity or concentration problems. Do not assume that all the problems which may arise reflect either the Attention Deficit Disorder or the inadequacy of the medicine. There is no medicine that makes any child a perfect child, and we doubt that any of us, if we consider it seriously for a moment, would want such a thing.

Approximately 50 percent of all prescribed medicine is not taken the way it is prescribed. This runs all the way from never filling the prescription in the first place to taking the medicine, but not in accordance with the doctor's instructions. Since it happens so often, this probably reflects something about human nature that will never change. But we should be aware of the problems that these habits might lead to when giving medicine to children with ADD.

How Do You Tell a Child Why He's Taking the Medication?

Children should know why they are taking medicine. Unfortunately, too often, when asked why they take Ritalin, Cylert, or Dexadrine, children answer saying, "Because I'm bad," or "It helps me be good." It is possible to explain to a child that the medicine has an effect on his behavior without adding to his feelings of inadequacy and without making him feel that drugs are a way to control behavior.

It is sufficient to tell most children that they have trouble paying attention and this causes them to have difficulty concentrating and getting their work done at home and in school. The medicine is useful because it helps them pay attention better and finish their work. This should be an adequate explanation even for the child who has a moderate behavior problem with poor impulse control. Under no circumstances would we ever suggest lying to a child or even taking advantage of his innocence and subtly misleading him. However, there is little advantage to be gained by explaining in detail to a young child that the medicine also helps with impulse control and will help keep him out of trouble. He will be quite aware that it's easier to get his work done and will become increasingly aware that he gets along better with other people. A similar explanation about the effect of the medication on impulse control or "acting without thinking" is helpful. These experiences can be combined in discussions with your child in a way that makes him feel that he can take greater credit for the positive things that are happening and that the medicine is simply a little bit of help to get him started.

Attention Deficit Disorder and Diet

There are two points of view regarding diet and Attention Deficit Disorder. The most popular follows the writings of Benjamin Feingold, a California pediatrician, who wrote a popular book for parents, *Why Your Child Is Hyperactive*. Based on his clinical experience, Feingold recommended that artificial flavors and colors, along with preservatives, refined sugar, and natural salicylates, be removed from a child's diet. He claimed this helped a large number of children with ADD. The other approach to diet is that of the orthomolecular psychiatrists. It is their belief that there is a biochemical imbalance and an insufficiency of naturally needed chemicals in the brains of many people, including children with Attention Deficit Disorder, hyperactivity, and learning disabilities, and that the way to remedy this is with a prescription of large doses of vitamins, most commonly vitamins C, B-3, and B-6. Orthomolecular psychiatrists believe that such vitamin deficiencies also underlie many serious mental disorders, such as schizophrenia.

Although there are Feingold societies throughout the United States and Canada and a number of cookbooks have been prepared describing additive-free diets, there is virtually no scientific evidence that such diets help even a handful of children with ADD. Nonetheless, because it is such a popular notion, it is worth discussing a bit more fully. Many parents of children with ADD have noticed that when their children eat especially large amounts of sweets at Halloween, Christmas, or Easter, their behavior becomes even more uncontrollable. So, although there is no scientific proof that refined sugar and artificial substances cause hyperactivity or attention problems, there are so many reports from parents that we cannot ignore them. Unfortunately, the observation that large amounts of sweets make children with ADD worse can be easily misinterpreted. It does not follow from what we have just discussed that, therefore, if you take all the sugars out of your hyperactive child's diet, you will necessarily cure him. It may be that many, many people are sensitive to immense amounts of refined sugar, but that certainly does not mean that too much refined sugar caused the problem in the first place. Just because two facts are connected doesn't mean one caused the other. After all, because you take an aspirin when you have a headache, and the aspirin works, does not prove that you got a headache because your body needed aspirin.

We are satisfied that research and extensive clinical experience have shown that sugar does not cause Attention Deficit Disorder. Sugar apparently can, however, make matters worse for some children with ADD. The relationship between eating sugar and changes in behavior is complex, and the results of research are contradictory. For example, researchers at one medical center in Pittsburgh reported recently that no matter how much sugar most children with ADD eat, it caused no change in their behavior. On the other hand, Keith Connors, who has done extensive work on diet and ADD over the years and is the author of the book *Food Additives and Hyperactive Children,* reported at a 1986 meeting of the American Psychological Association that the effect of sugar on a child's behavior depended on what else the child had eaten recently. Children who had fasted or eaten high-protein diets were not affected, no matter how much sugar they ate. Children who had just completed high-carbohydrate meals, however, showed a definite reaction to the sugar, and the quality of their behavior deteriorated.

There have been a few reports in medical journals of children responding favorably to changes in diet. It has been our practice to inform parents of the current status of medical and psychological opinion in this area and not discourage parents if they want to use a Feingold-type diet. The diet is difficult and expensive to implement because many of the necessary foods are not readily available in most supermarkets. But, although there is no reason to expect it to work, it is not a dangerous diet. In many ways it is as healthful as or, perhaps, even more so than the regular diet most people follow, so even if it doesn't help with hyperactivity and attention problems, it is a nutritious way to eat. We try to be very careful to avoid encouraging parents to use the diet, however. It is easy to fail or give up on it. The best that can be said about additive-free diets at this point is that they are not harmful, but they do not seem to work. However, if you want to give it a try in your house, there is no reason not to.

The same advice cannot be given about orthomolecular treatment because it is necessary to give your child large doses of vitamins. Since vitamin therapy is totally without any firm scientific support, there seems little reason to use it, and it should not be attempted without a careful discussion with your child's doctor. Some children do have vitamin deficiencies; some children do require large doses of vitamins for other reasons. But we are not aware of any evidence, except for the reports of a few orthomolecular psychiatrists on the basis of their own experience, that large doses of vitamins help children with ADD or hyperactivity.

A five-year collaborative study by the Board of Directors of the Canadian Mental Health Association strongly suggests no therapeutic effect from vitamin B treatment. Several years ago, the American Psychiatric Association published a report, "Megavitamin and Orthomolecular Therapy in Psychiatry." After reviewing the history and literature relating to this subject, the members of the committee concluded, "In our view, the results and claims of the advocates of megavitamin therapy have not been confirmed by several groups of psychiatrists and psychologists experienced in psychopharmacological research." Thus, the claims the megavitamin proponents made as far back as 1957 have not been confirmed. The committee concludes, "Under these circumstances, this task force considers the massive publicity which they promulgate using catch phrases which are really misnomers like megavitamin therapy and orthomolecular treatment to be deplorable."

Attention Deficit Disorder and Allergies

Medical reports and clinical evidence indicate there is a higher incidence of a number of different allergies in children with ADD. There does not seem to be a connection between any particular kind of allergy and ADD, but more children with ADD have allergies. In fact, this was one of the observations that led Feingold to suggest that children with ADD are physiologically more sensitive and have to be more careful about what substances they are exposed to.

The observations that have been made connecting allergies with ADD and hyperactivity do not, in any way, suggest that one causes the other. They may both be caused by, or connected to, a third factor, as yet unknown, or not connected at all. Furthermore, knowing this relationship has not assisted us in any practical way, because it does not give us guidance about any specific therapy. At this time, the importance of the apparent connection between allergies and ADD lies in the possibility that this information may lead, through further research, to better means of treating both disorders.

Several medicines used by allergists to treat a number of different problems, but primarily asthma, may cause symptoms similar to those of Attention Deficit Disorder. Antihistamines make some children more active. The bronchial dilator theophyllin is claimed to have a variety of side effects, including nervousness, restlessness, insomnia, and irritability. In one recent study, children with mild asthma were divided into two groups. One group received theophyllin, the other a placebo. Although parents were unable to note any changes in the children's behavior and there was no evidence on psychological tests that they were affected, teachers were consistently able to tell which children were receiving the drug and which the placebo. The children on the medication were described as more irritable, more active, less able to deal with unstructured time, and easily distracted from work. The results of this study, taken together with several others, offer support for the observation that the side effects of certain commonly used drugs may cause behaviors that mimic the symptoms of Attention Deficit Disorder in some children.

Of particular concern is the question of how to medically treat the allergic child who also has Attention Deficit Disorder. There have been no studies to show whether youngsters with ADD are any more sensitive to theophyllin or other drugs, but to our knowledge, there have been no reports to indicate the use of bronchial dilators cannot go on at the same time as use of the medicines used to treat ADD.

Managing the behavior of a child with ADD who is asthmatic can become complex. This is made more difficult by the fact that often a pediatric allergist may treat the child's asthma, and a pediatrician or child psychiatrist the ADD. It is essential that you make clear to your doctor, or both doctors, the nature of your child's symptoms and observe to see whether the symptoms are made worse by the use of theophyllin or other drugs. Do not make any adjustment in the medication yourself. Consult with your doctors and be patient. Because of the nature of these two disorders it often takes time to get a clear-cut picture of what causes each symptom and what is the best plan of medical treatment.

Medication and Later Drug Abuse

Drug abuse is a serious problem, and the question whether use of long-term medication to help control behavior early in a child's life might lead to later drug abuse is one that must be addressed. Fortunately, the results of several careful experiments following children over a long period of time are very reassuring. So far, no one has found that taking Ritalin, or any other drug to control ADD and hyperactivity, causes problems with drugs later in life. In fact, two interesting studies by researchers in the Department of Psychiatry at the University of Iowa and at Detroit's Lafayette Clinic suggest that just the opposite is true.

The Iowa research workers studied 51 boys who had been referred to their clinic because of hyperactivity, learning difficulties, and behavior problems. Twenty-six of the boys were given a trial of stimulant medication, while 25 received just short-term behaviorally oriented counseling. The children were between the ages of 6 and 12 when first seen and were followed up 5 years later, when they were 11 to 17 years old. The researchers were interested in a number of questions, but one of the most important was to assess the relationship between use of stimulant medication and drug abuse. They found a relationship, but it was opposite to what we might have feared. Unmedicated subjects, those who had not received stimulant medication, were significantly more likely to report that their friends asked them to smoke marijuana, and they were significantly more likely to report that they had actually tried marijuana. Another finding, although not statistically significant, was that in the previous month more unmedicated subjects experimented with tranquilizers and had more drinks of alcohol at one time than the children who had been given stimulant drugs.

Keep in mind, in this experiment two groups of children with ADD were being compared. But the results of the study still clearly answer the question of whether using stimulant drugs causes any drug problems later on. In fact, it may be that denying the stimulant medicine to the 25 children who received only behaviorally oriented counseling may have led to greater interpersonal difficulties and more unhappiness for them over the years, and this, in turn, might have been related to their drug misuse.

Use of Drugs During School Holidays and on Weekends

As in all questions about the use of medicine, your child's physician should be the final authority for decisions about drug dosage. Here, we will discuss briefly some considerations that go into making decisions about whether a child should continue on stimulants during school holidays and weekends. The medications we are reviewing here have a very short active life in a child's body. Three to four hours after Ritalin is taken, the therapeutic effect is gone, although traces of the drug remain in the child's system for a considerable period of time. Though there is some disagreement in this area, in general it is believed that the medicine has little, if any, cumulative effect, which means that a dose of Ritalin at 7:30 on Monday morning is equally effective, whether or not the child has taken the medicine continually throughout the weekend. This is, of course, different from the use of many medicines you may be familiar with. If you have an infection and are taking an antibiotic, you must adhere strictly to the schedule of drug administration, or subsequent doses may be less effective. So decisions about whether to continue Ritalin over the weekend or during school holidays usually depend pretty much on how the child behaves without the medicine.

There are some children for whom there is an advantage to giving the medicine seven days a week. We refer here to the child whose behavior differs so much when he is off the medicine that he becomes bewildered or frustrated by the dramatic differences in his own behavior. For example, one 10-year-old boy told us, "I can't stand it on the weekend. I know that I should be able to do things and to pay attention and to control my own behavior, but I can't. I can't stand it."

We would prefer to help the child recognize the nature of his disorder and learn to live with the problem, but some children are troubled more than others and, in those cases where the child himself describes his distress in such dramatic terms, consideration ought to be given to administering the medicine throughout the entire week. We are very cautious, of course, about encouraging children to look to medication as a solution for their problems or allowing children to become so dependent on medicine or other forms of help that they lose the motivation to seek ways to deal with their problems themselves. This is, without question, a thorny dilemma, but the option of using medication in this way should be kept open in a limited number of cases.

As with any drug that might be taken for a long period of time, it is a common-sense rule that the fewer pills a child takes, the better, even in the case of relatively safe medication, such as the psychostimulants. The simplest rule for deciding whether to use the medicine on, say, the weekend, is to see if the family and the child with ADD can manage without it. If they can, then do not use it. It might be necessary on occasion to use medicine on the weekend, although not on a regular schedule.

For example, your child may need medicine Sunday morning before church. Or there may be a family gathering Saturday evening that overwhelms the child unless he has had his medicine. This use is often appropriate, but, again, we caution you that if you wish to use Ritalin or Cylert or Dexadrine in this way, you should discuss it first with the physician who prescribed it. The general advice we offer in a chapter such as this is intended to alert you to the issues involved in order to broaden your understanding of what is happening with your child, but specific medical decisions require your doctor's consultation, as he or she knows your child's individual needs.

Many children who take Ritalin regularly through the school year can manage without it during the summer. Other children are better off taking the medication in the summer, too, because they are so impulsive or so active as to seriously interfere with the quality of their social relationships with other children their age, or to disrupt the family to such an extent that the negative psychological consequences are severe. In other words, it is usually best to try to get by without stimulants during the summer or over long vacations, such as the Christmas holiday. However, if your child cannot manage and his life is a disaster without it, then, of course, the best plan is to continue with the medicine.

When Should You Ask the Doctor
About Discontinuing Medication?

The decision to stop giving a child stimulant medication is a complex one. A number of factors have to be taken into consideration. Perhaps most important is the realization that it often is not possible to determine in advance if a child will be able to manage satisfactorily without medication. In most cases, a carefully controlled trial, either on holidays, as we have just discussed, or at other times, is the best way to find out. This should always be done in consultation with your child's physician. We realize that keeping up with the schedule of administering medicine to a child every day is very difficult.

Many people find it hard to stick to the specified schedule for taking the medicine they need. It is estimated that 50 percent of adult patients do not take medication as prescribed. For children these figures might be worse. Even in cases where children have to take medicine such as antibiotics for only a short time, say 10 days, many patients stop their medicine early. It was discovered in one study that 56 percent of patients had stopped taking such medicine by the third day, 71 percent by the sixth day, and 82 percent by the ninth day. In another study, researchers found that only 7.3 percent of 300 pediatric patients completed their course of antibiotics for ear infections.

Many parents appear to change the administration of their child's stimulant medicine or discontinue it without consultation with their physician. Often this is done because patients do not fully understand what the medicine is supposed to do and why it has to be continued for such a long time. In a recent study at the Children's Hospital of Eastern Ontario in Canada, the following results were obtained when patients with ADD who were taking Ritalin were followed over a period of 10 months. Twenty percent of the patients had stopped using the medicine by the end of the fourth month. By the end of the tenth month, only 55 percent of the children were still taking their prescribed medicine. Less than 10 percent of the families consulted their physicians prior to terminating the medication.

It is tempting to discontinue the medicine after your child has been taking it for a long time. In some cases there are no immediate changes in the child's behavior or, if there are changes, they occur in school or are covered up by other events in the child's life. Most parents who stop giving their child medicine do not, on their own, start it again. We regard figures such as we have just cited with considerable concern. As we have observed many times, management of children with ADD is difficult and frustrating. It is made even more complicated and troublesome when decisions such as discontinuing medicine are made without careful medical consideration.

Although the most common medication error parents make is to neglect to give medicine consistently, there is another mistake parents and teachers often make together. A teacher may observe that a child who had been doing quite well on medicine seems gradually, over a period of several weeks or even months, to have gotten back into old habits or patterns of behavior. It looks as if the medicine is no longer working.

Now it would be a rare teacher or parent who would ever suggest that a child take medicine that had not been prescribed by a physician, but it is not unusual for a parent, or parent and teacher, deciding together, to stop giving prescribed medicine without consultation with the doctor. So, in the case of the child just mentioned, medication is discontinued to see what effect that has on the child's behavior. If the child does not get worse, the parent and teacher may come to the mistaken conclusion that the medicine must not have been doing anything because the child is no worse off when you stop the medicine than he was when he was taking it.

Such an observation might be true, but the conclusion that the medicine is not helping is frequently an error. Children may need *increased* amounts of medication for several reasons. As their body size grows, they may need a larger dose. Some children's bodies get used to certain doses of medicine, so they need a higher dose in order to continue to benefit from it. Parents and teachers who think they have done a scientific experiment to evaluate the effectiveness of medicine have actually been led to a false conclusion. The reason the child's behavior does not deteriorate further when the medicine is discontinued is because the medicine was already at too low a level to provide any benefit. So the fact that the child's behavior showed no change when the medicine was stopped was not a true measure of the medicine's effectiveness.

In most cases parents do not discuss with the child's doctor the decision to stop giving medicine, or it may be mentioned the next time the child is in the doctor's office because of an illness or a routine checkup. In our example the student usually completes the school year without medication, and it may not be until the following fall, when the first teacher conferences occur or the first report cards come out, that any alarm is raised about how badly the child is doing. Then, with appropriate medical and psychological follow-up, the child is usually placed back on medicine at the appropriately adjusted dose that is necessary to give the same benefit that had been evident earlier in the preceding year. Sometimes it takes several years for the child to get back on medicine because parents carry in the back of their minds the idea that the medication was not effective, so they do not bring it up again with their doctor.

There are two simple steps to take when a child who has responded to medicine in the past no longer seems to benefit from it. First, check and make sure the child is taking the medicine the way it has been prescribed. Second, recognize that medicine's failure to continue to do the job is often an indication that the dose is now too low. The proper experiment for parents to try, if permitted by the doctor, is to give a higher dose to see if that results in an improvement in the child's behavior, rather than to discontinue the medicine.

When Children Refuse to Take Medication

Reluctance or outright refusal to take medication occurs frequently among teenagers but at times is a problem even for children as young as 9 or 10. There are three main reasons. For many, refusal is a continuation of the battle for control between parents and child. Younger children can often be forced to take their medicine. However, in the case of a teenager whose relationship with parents has deteriorated to the point where there are constant battles for supremacy and control, there is little parents can do to force compliance. The greater the effort they make to get the child to take medicine, the more resistance they encounter.

The second reason children refuse medication is social pressure. This problem occurs most often when a child has to take medicine while in school, because children do not want to be different. Even in those cases where a child is not teased and others may not even know about the medication, the child's self-conscious feelings and fears about what his friends might think about him are sufficient to make him resist the medication.

The third reason children refuse medication is more subtle and complex. Some children say simply, "I don't need medicine. There's nothing wrong with me." Efforts to explain to the child the nature of the Attention Deficit Disorder and problems it creates in behavior and learning are usually met with either an argument or flat denial. A child may say, "I can pay attention if I want to."

In such a case we have to be mindful that the child is not insisting there is nothing wrong with him because he feels so good about himself, or because he is ignorant of the fact that his schoolwork is a problem or that his behavior is difficult. Rather the child is only too aware that there is something wrong, and he finds the idea so upsetting or threatening that he refuses even to acknowledge it. Usually the more threatened by the disorder the child feels, the more vehement become his denials that there is anything wrong with him. It is easy to see that efforts to convince him that he does indeed have a problem usually meet with failure because they only add to the child's distress, make him more anxious, and cause him to erect an even more impenetrable barrier to keep from recognizing the truth.

In most cases we have found that children arrive at this position only after a number of years during which the Attention Deficit Disorder was either undiagnosed or misunderstood. In one way or another, parents and teachers have unintentionally caused the child to view himself as inadequate or a failure. When children deny that they have ADD even in the face of careful explanations about it, we have to ask why they are running from the truth. The most common reason is that they have been made to feel especially bad about themselves over the years, through misdiagnosis, misunderstanding, or improper management at home or at school.

Most children can be persuaded to take medication if we take the time to understand their refusal and deal with the underlying problems first. In the case of the child who is too frightened to acknowledge that there is something wrong with him, this may take quite a bit of time to resolve. Once the child comes to the point where he can accept his limitations and understand why he resists facing the Attention Deficit Disorder, then the issues of medical compliance and taking medicine on schedule can be dealt with more easily.

Side Effects

Parents should be concerned about the side effects of any medicine. Short-term side effects resulting from the use of stimulants may include insomnia, decreased appetite, weight loss, abdominal pain, and headaches. Only in a minority of children do side effects such as these occur, and they tend to be minor and temporary. If, however, they are severe or last longer than several days, you should discuss them with your child's physician.

Stimulant medication makes some children irritable and whiny. Although this occurs in fewer than 5 percent of children treated with psychostimulants, the problem can be severe enough that medication has to be discontinued. Usually these side effects are evident immediately; in some cases they do not appear until the dose is increased later on in treatment. Whether to continue treating a child with medication in such circumstances is a difficult decision. In many cases there is minimal benefit from the medicine, and in those cases the decision to discontinue is easy. For other children, the medicine works as it is supposed to; the child concentrates better, is less active, and is less impulsive. Nonetheless, the irritability and fussiness may be more than parents can tolerate.

If a child experiences these side effects with one of the stimulants, it is possible that they may not occur with another. For that reason, it is usually a good idea to switch to other medications for careful trials as well before giving up on the idea of medication treatment.

There is a relationship between age and the side effects of irritability and whininess. These symptoms are much more common in children younger than five years of age. Many children who display a variety of side effects, including increased irritability, when first given medication at age three, four, or even five, are able when they are older to take the medicine, benefit from it, and not show any side effects.

There is only limited information available about significant long-term side effects of stimulants. One long-term side effect parents often ask about is possible decrease of growth rate. A number of studies were published in the late 1960's and early 1970's suggesting that long-term use of high doses of stimulants, particularly Dexadrine and Ritalin, caused a slowdown in children's growth rates. However, a recent review of all published literature by a panel of the Food and Drug Administration suggests that any height and weight suppression occurs only for the first year or two of therapy; there does not seem to be any long-term effect on ultimate growth. We have discussed previously the question of whether there is a tendency for children who have been treated with stimulants to become abusers of drugs in later life.

3 Behavioral Management

This chapter on behavioral management begins with a discussion of a number of principles that give us guidance in understanding how behavior, both good and bad, is learned and how it can be changed. These principles have come to be called "behavioral" because the emphasis is on observable behavior with no special concern about feelings and attitudes beneath the surface. It would be wrong, of course, to think we can ignore a person's feelings and pay attention to only his behavior, but at times it is useful to make the distinction because it makes our task of managing children easier and more straightforward. The latter portion of this chapter will deal with the practical application of these principles.

Overview

This first section is divided into several parts. First will be the review of basic principles of how behavior and habits are learned, followed by the principles of behavior change and behavior modification. We will describe a step-by-step program for behavior change that will include methods for increasing desirable behavior and methods for decreasing undesirable behavior. There are some good things we want our children with ADD to do more of, and some bad things we want them to stop. Next will follow a review of ways in which children with ADD differ from other children in how they learn. We will conclude Chapter 3 by integrating all this information in a way that leads to some very practical guidance in the day-to-day management of your youngster with ADD.

Behavior Principles

After reading several paragraphs of this section you might be tempted to skip ahead, because what you are reading will seem no more than common sense. We urge you to continue reading anyway. It is true that much of what we will discuss here will be familiar to some extent. Nonetheless, we have found that these principles of learning and habit formation have to be understood in considerable detail if we are to apply them effectively with children with ADD. The reasons for this will become clear when we move into the next section, on how children with ADD learn. Often only subtle or very small errors in the way we set up a behavior management program for a youngster with ADD account for failure. There is a very thin line between success and failure, and we want to make sure we do everything possible to increase the chances for success.

There are only a few principles of learning with which we need to be concerned. Before we go ahead with them, several definitions are necessary. First is the term *behavior*. We all know in general what the word means, but it is important for us to have a specific understanding. Too often parents think they are describing behavior, but it is not behavior they are talking about at all. For example, we often ask parents what behaviors of their child with ADD irritate them most. We will frequently hear a response such as, "He is so angry and mean with his little sister." Now, on further questioning it becomes clear that the parents know exactly what behaviors they are referring to, but "anger" is not a behavior, it is a feeling, and saying a child is "mean" to his sister is an interpretation of what the person is doing. We usually follow parents' statements with a question such as, "Tell me what specific behaviors you see your child doing that cause you to say that he is angry or being mean." This results in the parents' response describing the behavior, not attitudes or feelings. For example, the child may hit his younger sister. He may make angry faces or say nasty things. These are behaviors.

There are times when the words used to describe a child sound like behaviors, but, even then, we cannot be sure a person is actually describing behavior instead of offering an interpretation or opinion. For example, we frequently speak to parents or teachers who say that a child is hyperactive or, simply, overactive. That is a description of behavior. But it is usually necessary to go a step further and ask exactly what sorts of behaviors do you see that cause you to say he is hyperactive? Different behavior and different people sometimes result in different definitions of hyperactivity. For instance, an impatient, intolerant, or passive teacher might interpret normal exuberance and enthusiasm in a kindergarten child as hyperactivity. That is why it is important that we describe the behavior itself. That is the starting place. We all have to be talking about the same thing in order to communicate clearly and to set up the best behavior management program.

Two other technical words require definition — *reinforcement* and *extinction*. A reinforcement or reinforcer is usually a reward. The terms refer to anything that increases or reinforces the probability that a certain behavior will occur or increase in frequency. So we can reinforce a child's cooperative behavior with a younger sibling by giving him a tangible reward, such as a toy or a piece of candy, or an intangible reward, such as love or praise. This latter sort of reinforcer is often more potent than tangible reinforcement. Saying to your child, "That makes me proud," or "I'm very pleased to see what you did with your brother, Fred," is an intangible reinforcement. Much reinforcement comes from outside the child and is provided by parents, teachers, or other children. Some reinforcement, however, is intrinsic. This means it comes from within the person himself, or the act that we want him to do is rewarding in and of itself. Many types of success are intrinsically rewarding. The jogger who increases his distance from one to two miles may feel very proud of himself and be motivated to get out the next day and do it again simply because he has reached a goal he set for himself and feels reinforced. He does not require an audience to tell him how well he has done. Similarly, the child who takes a cookie from the cookie jar when his mother isn't watching has that behavior reinforced or rewarded by eating a tasty cookie. Punching a younger brother or sister and causing a cry of pain may please a jealous child with ADD who feels rejected and treated worse than the younger child. The reinforcement or reward that comes from the pleasure of revenge on the younger child may be very powerful and cause the punching behavior to continue even in the face of parents' strong disapproval or punishment. In other words, the reward the child gets from the behavior is more powerful than the punishment that the parents use to eliminate the behavior. That is why it is so important to understand the nature of the reinforcement. It helps us understand why certain behavior persists even when, to us as adults looking at the behavior and our response to it, we think it is so illogical or nonsensical. One of the first steps to changing behavior is to understand why it is reinforcing to the child.

Lying provides a good example. Why do children persist in lying, for example, about incomplete schoolwork, when they know you are going to find out the truth sooner or later? When that finally happens the child must know he will be in twice the trouble, because now it is not just the incomplete schoolwork that upsets you, but the lies that were told, as well.

Try to examine these events from the child's point of view to see what reinforces lying. Your child probably fears your response if he confesses to unfinished assignments. You may insist the child stays in the house until the work is done. More importantly, you will probably get angry. Your anger makes him upset and nervous. By lying, he avoids your displeasure; avoiding your anger makes him less anxious; escape from anxiety is a very good feeling. Reduction of anxiety will reinforce just about any behavior. That is why your child lies. Judgment day is off in the future, anxiety is now. The lie reduces anxiety, so the habit becomes stronger. It may make no sense to you at the moment, but viewed from a behavioral perspective with an understanding of reinforcement principles, the lies are a logical consequence of the circumstances.

No behavior will continue if it is not reinforced. The reason bad habits persist or annoying behavior continues, even when we attempt to discourage it, is because it is being reinforced in some way that we do not fully understand. If we eliminate all reinforcement, the behavior will cease. This process is referred to as *extinction*. In other words, we can extinguish undesirable behavior by taking care to see to it the behavior is never rewarded or reinforced. This is an easy principle to state, but in real life figuring out, first, all the things that reinforce the behavior and, second, ways in which to ensure that the behavior will not be reinforced are far more complex and difficult.

In discussing the preceding definitions, we have introduced several principles of learning that are the foundation for what we know about learning behavior and habit formation. The principles can be stated concisely. Behavior must be reinforced or it won't be learned. Once behavior is learned, if you eliminate all reinforcement, eventually the behavior will extinguish.

There are several other principles that should be noted. Behavior that is learned on a partial reinforcement schedule is more resistive to extinction than behavior learned with 100 percent reinforcement. An illustration should make this clear. Consider a four-year-old-child put to bed at 8:30 p.m. with some mild protest. The child's bedroom is down the hall from the living room where both parents are sitting reading or watching television. The child knows he risks a stern reprimand from his parents and possibly a smack on the rear end if he comes out into the living room, but he does not want to be in bed, so he has to find a way to delay sleep and get his parents' attention. He calls for a drink of water. In this example, as soon as he asks for a drink the first time, his mother goes into the kitchen, gets him a glass of water, and brings it to him; he drinks it, and having accomplished his purpose, he settles down and eventually goes to sleep. But he has learned a powerful lesson. So the following night he does the same thing and his mother responds in the same way. As soon as he speaks up, she brings him his glass of water. In a very short time the ritual of asking for and receiving a glass of water is firmly established, and the child does it every night. His mother is mildly irritated by it, but she can live with it.

Consider another hypothetical family. The same circumstances apply. This family too includes a four-year-old child who doesn't like his 8:30 bedtime. This second child's parents, however, have a different approach to managing his bedtime delays. When he begins to call for a glass of water, both father and mother ignore him. They know that if you ignore him long enough, eventually, he will stop nagging. Unfortunately, repeated requests for water coming from the bedroom down the hall are irritating and disruptive. Sometimes the parents can ignore him just fine, but other times it is easier, after he has asked for water a half dozen times, to finally give in and give it to him just to quiet him down. This second child, like his age-mate we described before, also learns an effective technique for delaying bedtime, and the ritual of getting him a glass of water soon becomes established in his life as well.

The first child asked for a glass of water and the reinforcement or reward (his mother's attention and the glass of water) occurred every time. We say this habit was learned at a 100 percent rate of reinforcement. The second child might have called for a glass of water 10 times before his mother appeared at his bedside. This child had to work 10 times as hard. He knows he will not get a glass of water every time he asks for it. He may now know that he has been reinforced 10 percent of the time, but he does know that sometimes he will ask for a glass of water and he will not get anything. He has learned how to get water, but he has learned something else as well; he has learned persistence. This second child has learned his habit with a partial reinforcement schedule.

Most human behavior is learned through partial reinforcement schedules. And behavior learned through partial reinforcement is much harder to extinguish than behavior learned under 100 percent reinforcement. The reason is quite simple, and we can understand it if we consider again the two thirsty children we have just discussed. Imagine that both sets of parents now decide that things have gone far enough and they are fed up with the bedtime-drink ritual. They are going to break their child of the habit. The parents of the first child resolve staunchly to, first, advise him that there will be no more drinks after getting into bed, and then commit themselves firmly to remain in the living room and not respond to the child's requests for water. If the family is typical, their youngster responds to their explanation of the new rule about as well as everybody else's child; he doesn't pay any attention to it at all. The request for water may be a bit delayed that night after the imposition of the new rule, but, sure enough, eventually it comes. The parents hang on and ignore him and after a few more requests he settles down and eventually falls asleep. The parents may know that the battle has not been won, but they know they are on the right track. Comes the next night and the child tries again. The parents hang on. The third and fourth nights follow and perhaps by the fourth or fifth night the child does not ask for water at all. He may try again a week later, but if the parents are consistent, eventually the behavior extinguishes. The parents have removed all reinforcement.

The parents of our second child try exactly the same thing. But they have a problem that the first family did not have. Their child has already learned persistence. The first child had not. He was used to getting reinforced every time. As soon as he was no longer getting his water, he knew things had changed. It was worth it to him to keep trying; after all, it did not take much energy to call out again for a glass of water, but it pretty soon became clear that it would not work and so he stopped. The second child, however, is used to working hard. Sometimes he has had to call for water 10, 15, even 20 times. Some nights he does not get water at all. But he knows that if he keeps at it, eventually he is going to get what he wants. And that's what he does!

It is not uncommon for a child who has learned his habit on a partial reinforcement schedule to ask for water 10, 20, even 50 times that first night. Perhaps his parents are wise enough and strong enough and in sufficient control of their own frustration to not respond. Unfortunately, after a child calls out from his room 50 times over the course of an hour or two, most parents lose faith in their plan about ignoring the behavior and eventually go in to talk to him. They may, unwisely, give him water to finally shut him up because "anything is better than having the whole evening ruined" or they may simply go into his bedroom and tell him that they are not going to give him water. They may go into his room and give him a spanking or reprimand him severely. Either of these two choices is unfortunate. In both cases the child has successfully captured his parents' attention, and he is calling the tune, not they. If the parents spank or otherwise severely reprimand, they antagonize the child, arouse him further, and interfere with the relaxation that should precede sleep. Additionally, heated feelings develop, frustration builds, and parents feel guilty and angry. The example could be taken further. It should be clear by this time that if this second family wants to extinguish the bedtime water-drinking behavior, they are going to have to work at it a lot longer than the first family, simply because the child has learned to persevere.

It is often during an attempt to eliminate behavior that parents actually change the reinforcement schedule to such a low proportion level that they are actually making the behavior even harder to extinguish. This occurs when parents have firmly resolved not to give in, but eventually do. In a case like this, what they have taught their child is an even greater degree of perseverance. Whereas he might have been used to getting rewarded $\frac{1}{10}$ of the time, now he learns that he only gets rewarded $\frac{1}{100}$ of the time, but if he persists, eventually he will get his way. So there is a very simple principle that emerges from all of this, in addition to the one about schedules of reinforcement, and that is simply this: do not start an extinction program unless you are prepared to see it through.

Distinction Between Punishment and Extinction

Punishment for undesirable behavior suppresses that behavior but does not, under most conditions, eliminate it. The process of extinction is a more systematic means of eliminating undesirable behavior. Also punishment is usually connected in the child's mind with the punisher, so a child may stop an undesirable behavior when the person who gives him the spanking is around but not at other times. Punishment also causes fear. If a child is punished too much, he may not only stop doing what you want him to stop, which is fine, but also come to fear you in a way you do not want. The same thing happens in school when a young child learns to fear school or fear particular subjects because punishment has been connected with them. There is no such thing as healthy fear. It may be sensible to teach your young child to fear fire or heavy traffic, but try to avoid causing fear whenever possible.

There are other disadvantages too in the use of punishment. Punishment involves an aggressive act on the part of the parent directed toward the child. Children view their parents as models. They copy their behavior. There have been a number of studies which have examined the behavior of children whose parents have used physical punishment. Children who are spanked or otherwise punished with force show far more aggression with their friends as well as back toward their parents. An occasional single slap on the rear end may be part of normal child rearing, but when physical punishment goes beyond that, it is not only ineffective generally, but often creates more problems. An interesting example is that of the parent who spanks a child as punishment because the child has hit or otherwise hurt a brother or sister. What do you suppose a child learns from a parent who tells him, "Hitting a person is no way to solve your problem," at the same time the parent is hitting him? It is very confusing and hypocritical, and breeds angry resentment. The general rule is that children's aggression which is either accepted or physically punished will increase. Aggression must be extinguished in a systematic manner.

Parents of children with ADD are especially vulnerable to the use of physical punishment because the child with ADD causes so much frustration. Most parents admit they physically punish their children, not so much because it is good for the child, but because the parents become so angry and frustrated. Such acts may reduce the parents' frustration but usually do not help the child, and, in fact, usually harm him. If you cannot handle the frustration your child creates even with the procedures discussed in this book, talk to your family doctor. Perhaps psychological counseling will aid you in living with your child more harmoniously.

We recommend positive reinforcement and extinction as methods to change behavior and reserve punishment for those rare occasions it is necessary. There are times when the consequences of a child's behavior are so dangerous that we take the risk about hurting or frightening him. Take, for example, the impulsive child who dashes out into a busy street. This sort of behavior is best dealt with firmly and may require a spanking. Positive reinforcement for self-control and keeping out of the street is an important part of the management, but first consideration has to be given to the child's physical safety. Similarly, the 18- or 24-month-old child who insists on sticking metal objects into electric outlets has to be stopped for his own safety, even if this requires punishment. Care must be taken with any punishment that it not injure the child. Most spankings are best thought of as exclamation points that might sting a little bit on the rear end, but serve the primary purpose of emphasizing the parents' displeasure. There are absolutely no circumstances under which physical punishment should be used to get revenge or to cause the child sufficient pain so that it is the pain that the child seeks to avoid in the future, rather than the parents' disapproval.

Appropriate or desirable behavior must be reinforced immediately. This can't be stressed strongly enough. The principle is especially true during the initial stages of any behavior change process. During these initial stages desired behavior must be reinforced each time it is exhibited. This is a 100 percent reinforcement schedule. When the newly acquired behavior reaches a satisfactory level, it should be reinforced intermittently. As we have discussed, this will make the behavior more resistant to extinction. Tangible reinforcers are a good starting place, but they should soon be replaced with social reinforcers. Parents are often reluctant to give things to their children as rewards or reinforcers for desirable behavior. We have heard parents refer to this practice as "bribing" their children. If you will think about it for a moment, you will see that even the term "bribe" is inappropriate in this case. A bribe is actually something you give to a person for doing something wrong or dishonest. You try to bribe your way out of trouble when you have committed a crime. Giving a child a reward for doing something right is an excellent idea. When you get a reward for proper behavior or constructive behavior, you are more likely to do it again. Despite the fact that many of us enjoy the work we do, and it is intrinsically rewarding and reinforcing, how many of us would continue to go to our jobs day after day, year after year, if we did not receive a tangible reinforcer in the form of our wages or salary?

Still, we recognize that you cannot constantly give a child rewards for desirable behavior, and after the behavior becomes established, you should seek ways to substitute praise and encouragement for tangible reinforcers. We will discuss these procedures in a step-by-step manner later in this chapter.

Differences in the Learning of Children with ADD

The principles of learning and habit formation we have been discussing apply to all children. Nonetheless, there are some differences between the learning of children with ADD and others which have to be understood if we are to be most effective in managing their behavior at home and in the classroom. In this section we will discuss some of those differences before moving on to consider their practical application.

Reinforcement Schedules

Children with ADD, those with hyperactivity, and those with neither of these learn behaviors and habits equally well with 100 percent reinforcement. However, children with ADD are much less efficient learners on partial reinforcement schedules. The same rules about persistence of habits learned on partial reinforcement apply to children with ADD as to others, but when we consider how children learn behaviors and habits in the first place, we find that children with ADD have a marked disadvantage because it takes them longer to learn in most instances. This delay in learning has nothing to do with the child's intelligence. Some careful thought helps clarify why the child with ADD might learn more slowly.

In the early stages of any learning at home or in the classroom, the rules children must follow and the habits they must establish are not very clear to the child. If, every time a child makes a correct response, the parent or teacher says, "That's very good," then the child has clear direction about what he is supposed to do. In this way 100 percent reinforcement has the advantage of organizing things for the child. It helps to point out what he is supposed to pay attention to and to focus his attention. Consider, on the other hand, the child with ADD trying to learn a simple task in the classroom. The teacher is able to give him direct feedback or reinforcement only infrequently, a partial schedule of reinforcement. Unfortunately, the child with ADD is not always paying attention, even when the teacher gives the occasional reinforcement or direction. It is in this way that he suffers a learning handicap.

Timing of Reinforcement

Children with ADD learn just as well as other children when reinforcement is provided immediately. However, if there is a slight delay between the time the child does something and when he receives some feedback or reinforcement, the child with ADD learns much less efficiently than his non-ADD peer. The longer the interval between the time of the behavior and the time of the reinforcement, the less efficiently the child with ADD will learn. As in our example above, the reasons for this are probably complex and subtle, but there is one obvious feature that probably accounts for a lot of the difference between children with ADD and others. The longer the interval between the time the child exhibits the behavior and the time he gets some feedback about it, the more opportunity there is for his mind to skip to some other subject. So by the time the reinforcement comes, whether it is in the form of a tangible reward, praise from the teacher, or even feedback information that says, "That's good. You did it right," the child's mind may be on another subject.

The type of learning that we are talking about, day-to-day habits, behaviors, and school learning, actually consists of uncountable small segments and many, many repetitions of the same behavior over and over again. For example, it has been estimated that the average first-grade child uses each new word he encounters somewhere between

4,000 and 5,000 times in speech and reading exercises before it becomes firmly implanted in his mind. Considering these many, many experiences that add up to make the complete learning experience, it is not hard to imagine that the child with ADD is going to be at a disadvantage if he is paying less attention to the reinforcement than his classmate who sits across the aisle. There is a different, but closely related, aspect to how the reinforcement is presented to a child that we will discuss next.

Contingent Versus Non-contingent Reinforcement

Contingent reinforcement refers to the process whereby parent or teacher makes clear for the child what the reinforcement is for. At the end of the day, a first-grade teacher might say to a child, "You are behaving nicely, Billy." Alternately she may come up to him as he lines up at the door with his boots and coat on ready to go home and say, "Billy, I'm very pleased with the way you dressed yourself quickly and lined up here at the door and stood quietly waiting for the other children to get ready." In the latter case her kind words and praise are clearly made contingent on the behavior. The contingency or connection should be drawn clearly for the child. The child with ADD, once again, learns less efficiently if the contingency is not made explicit.

Who Paces the Task?

Many things we expect our children to do are governed by our own schedules. There are other things that children can schedule for themselves. Do children with ADD learn and perform more efficiently when they schedule their own work, or when we schedule it for them? There are two answers to this question, because it depends on the nature of the task. If the work is such that parent or teacher helps the child pay attention and organize his activities, then the child does better when someone else paces the task. For example, if children are taking a spelling test and the teacher says before giving each word, "All right now, class, the next word goes on line two, and should be started at the left-hand margin, and the spelling word is . . . ," the child with ADD will do as well as others in the classroom because the teacher's pacing of the task helps him organize it. If, however, the teacher's pacing of the task merely serves to force the child to do things on her schedule, then the child would be better off if he paced the task himself. He will not do as well as in our first example, but he will do better than if the adult forces his own schedule on the child.

Organization

Children with ADD are more erratic in their approach to solving problems. This can be illustrated with an example. Imagine a checkerboard with 64 squares. Two people play a game. The squares are numbered and person A has to guess which square person B is thinking of.

There's no trick to this game. Person A knows there are 64 squares. Even with the worst luck of all, A should not make more than 63 errors before guessing the correct square. The best way to ensure that you'll have no more than 63 errors is to approach the task systematically. Each square can be guessed in some organized way. Start with the rows—or with the columns—but work systematically. With 64 squares if you don't work systematically, chances are you might forget whether you've guessed one square, come back to it, and waste a turn.

Now think of your child with ADD. If he's 9 or 10 years old or older, it may be that this task would be quite easy for him and he, too, would make no more than 63 errors maximum. On the other hand, because of their difficulty in paying attention and because of their impulsivity, many children with ADD simply cannot organize a logical, systematic method of attack for even as simple a task as this. On the average, children with ADD tend to make more errors at this simple guessing game than do children who do not have Attention Deficit Disorder.

If a child finds it difficult to organize this task, imagine what it must be like when he hears his teacher say, "Put away your reading book, take out your arithmetic book and a clean sheet of paper and a pencil, turn to page 38, number your sheet of paper from 1 to 10 down the left-hand margin, and do every other problem on the page. Work carefully and neatly and do the even problems if you get done early."

Have you ever sent your youngster on an errand with instructions such as, "Go up to your room, get your plaid shirt, stop in my bedroom at the sewing basket and get me a needle and thread and a yellow thimble, meet me in the living room, and I'll sew on that button for you." You know the frustration you experience when, after sitting in the living room for 10 minutes, you go to your son's bedroom and find him sitting on his bed looking through a book or listening to the radio. He got as far as his room and then got distracted. In fact, he probably doesn't even remember what it was you asked him to do. "Oh yeah, I forgot," he says when you ask what he's doing. It's easy to misinterpret this sort of behavior as irresponsibility or even outright defiance. What usually happens, however, is that he was not paying careful attention in the first place and did not get all the directions, and his approach to the task is not much different from the random guessing that might occur in the guessing game with the checkerboard. Since he had no clear goals in mind when he got into his room, he was easily distracted by something else and was probably honestly surprised when you, quite angry, marched into his room and demanded to know what he has been doing while you have been waiting for him downstairs.

These observations on how youngsters with Attention Deficit Disorder learn, taken together, suggest not only some guidelines about how to organize their experiences and how to guide them, but also what limitations we have to place on our expectations for them. We should stress that parents often find these explanations of how children with ADD learn very frustrating. Unless you have seen large numbers of children and understand that these behaviors reflect actual physical inability to organize experiences and behavior, it is much too easy to dismiss them as bad habits or examples of poor character or selfishness. We often find, after explaining in detail to many parents the very things we have been discussing here, that the parents will nod their heads in acknowledgment, but then dismiss most of what we have said by commenting, "Well, that may all be true, but what it really comes down to is that he just wants things his own way."

It is sad when that happens and even frightening, because then it is easy to begin to view your child as your adversary and to look at your relationship with him as a constant battle with a winner and a loser. If that becomes the frame of reference in any family, it becomes a self-fulfilling prophecy, and the normal habits of getting along and living with each other often are turned into battles and the family home into a battleground. Unfortunately, if it reaches this level of conflict, there usually is no winner at all.

The Behavior Change Process

There are specific steps that should be taken in order to change behavior. As in earlier sections of this book, much of what we are going to discuss here may seem obvious. We caution you, however, not to treat these matters lightly or superficially just because it seems like common sense. The more careful attention you give to following these specific instructions, the more likely you are to have success.

The first step in the behavior change process is selecting which behavior you want to change. Remember our discussion and definition of behavior earlier. In order to change behavior, you must be able to describe it very clearly in such a way that another person would know exactly what you are talking about. It is not very helpful to say that you want to change your child's "attitude" or want to "make him more considerate" or "more responsible" in the way in which he does schoolwork or chores around the house. If a friend or neighbor looked at your child, it would be very hard for him to tell exactly what you meant by attitude, consideration, or responsibility. Rather, determine what behaviors your child engages in that cause you to call him inconsiderate or irresponsible or a child with a bad attitude. It is those behaviors that we want to change.

Generally we recommend, at the beginning, you work on only one individual behavior or a small group of behaviors at a time. Do not be impatient or unrealistic in your expectations. Often more is happening in these early stages than you realize. You are going to demonstrate to your child that you really have both the means to control his behavior and the commitment to do it. You are going to improve your credibility and effectiveness. You are going to convince yourself once again that you are capable of being a good parent and are able to manage your child's behavior. All of this can be accomplished by success in controlling only one or a small group of behaviors. The rest will come in time and will be accomplished more easily once the proper groundwork is laid.

The behavior you choose to modify does not have to be the most troublesome or the most dramatic behavior you want to change. Our criterion for choosing is to select behavior we think we can be successful in altering. We do this, first, because it is best to do the easy work at the beginning, and second, because success breeds success. So choose a behavior. It might be a temper tantrum. It might be disruption at the meal table. It could be interrupting when others are talking. Perhaps your five-year-old child chooses to make his most intrusive demands at the time you are on the telephone or in the bathroom or busy at the kitchen stove with a pot boiling over. You may want to discourage your eight-year-old from pulling his four-year-old sister's hair every time you are out of the room. Or, as one mother told us, "I think I'd be very happy with my life if he would just stop walking on the furniture and use the floor like everybody else."

All of these behaviors are easy to describe, and anyone watching your child would be able to tell whether he is doing it or not doing it. Furthermore, all of these behaviors are easy to count. You can count the number of times your child interrupts when you are on the telephone. You can add up the number of times your son pulls his sister's hair. Even if you do not keep formal records of how many times these things happen, you have a pretty good idea of how often they occur, so you will be able to tell whether you are having some effect once you begin the behavior change process.

There are several other considerations in selecting the target behavior for your first project. Choose behavior that occurs frequently. Behavior that is very disruptive but occurs only three or four times a year, even if it is very serious and dangerous behavior, probably should not be your primary concern at this point. Also, choose behavior over which you have some control. For example, you have control over a child's temper tantrum because you can pick him up, carry him to his room, leave him in there, and close and lock the door. It is much more difficult to control behavior when the child is primarily responsible for it. For example, if you want your child to get dressed faster, it is not as easy for you to impose your will on him as it is when he's having a temper tantrum. It is very difficult to "pull out" behavior from children. You know very well how obstructionistic children can be and how frustrating their passivity is when you want them to hurry up and do something because you are on a tight schedule. So, to start, choose behavior over which you have some control. This point will become clearer as we go along and discuss more examples.

Methods for Increasing Desirable Behavior

In this section, we will consider the application of some principles we have already learned. Simply put, the most important thing is to begin applying rewards or reinforcement for behaviors we want to improve. We know that we have to clearly identify the behavior and then select an appropriate reinforcer. The reinforcer has to be presented, initially, as close as possible to 100 percent of the time. It has to be contingent, that is, it has to be closely connected to the behavior, and then we have to find a way to switch from 100 percent reinforcement to partial reinforcement.

Step 1. Select the behavior you want to change. For purposes of illustration here, let us imagine you want to teach your seven-year-old child to sit quietly and not interrupt while the family is watching a half-hour television program.

Step 2. Select an appropriate reinforcer. There are an unlimited number of possible choices when it comes time to select what might be rewarding to a child. Some children can be rewarded with small amounts of food, such as candy or other kinds of treats. Some children are rewarded with colored stickers pasted on a sheet of paper. Some children may be rewarded by having 15 minutes of free time to do as they like. This choice is particularly effective as a reward in school classrooms. A very effective reward for young children is to tell them that they can earn 15 minutes of undivided attention from their mother or father and that you will do anything with them they like.

Step 3. Set up the rules. Explain carefully to your child what you want to be done. For example, in the case we are discussing here, tell him that you expect him to not interrupt from the time that the television program starts until the first commercial. When the program resumes, he has to keep quiet again until the next commercial. Then he has to keep quiet until the end of the program. He can leave the room, but he cannot interrupt. The same sort of rules can be set up for any sort of behavior. They can be applied to taking out the garbage, completing schoolwork assignments, or any other behavior that you want to increase in frequency and establish as a good habit. (There are limitations on how much can be accomplished with this procedure with children with ADD, but we can accomplish a great deal.)

Step 4. Explain to your child the connection between the rules and the reinforcer. Point out that you have been to the store and purchased a package of stickers of small, brightly colored animals.

Take a sheet of colored construction paper and mark it off into small squares. Make clear to your child that every time he is successful and doesn't interrupt your television viewing that you and he, together, will get a sticker from the package and put it on the sheet of paper. Notice how this procedure meets our requirement for a 100 percent reinforcement schedule and also for contingent reinforcement, because you are making very clear to the child exactly why you are doing what you are doing.

Step 5. Explain what happens next. For many young children, selecting and pasting the stickers is sufficient reward itself. You might, however, allow your child to qualify for a slightly larger prize when he has collected 10, 15, or 20 stickers. So tell him when 20 stickers have been pasted on the page, you will take him to the store and buy him a small present, say, something for a dollar or less. Keep in mind that your child may not be successful every time. He may still interrupt.

In the early stages it is very important that you make every effort to help him be successful. If, for example, you notice out of the corner of your eye that your child is going to interrupt and ruin his chance for a sticker during that segment of the television program, put your arm around him and put your finger across your pursed lips in order to remind him to keep quiet. Eventually we want him to do this on his own, but, at first, we have to make sure that he achieves some success. If he makes an error and interrupts and does not earn a sticker for one particular segment, do not make a fuss about it. It is not necessary to remind him that he did not get his sticker for that time. Rather, the next time he's successful, give him a sticker and praise him. Continually remind him how well he is doing and how pleased you are with his progress. Minimize his failures.

Step 6. Modifying the procedures. Eventually it should be possible to reduce the need for tangible reinforcers, such as the stickers, and substitute two intangible rewards: your praise and the child's sense of satisfaction about a job well done. This might take a lot of time. Many parents find that, after they have achieved some success with the stickers, they become a bit sloppy and neglect to follow through as carefully as they should. This is often associated with an increase in the frequency of the undesirable behavior, in our example, interrupting. It is important that you step back and take a look at the procedures that you have gone through and where you might have begun to get a little sloppy or where you might have changed the procedures. Too often, at this point, parents misinterpret what has happened when the behavior recurs and simply think that the procedures "worked for a while, but then they didn't work any more." The procedures always work. The procedures will continue to be effective as long as they are implemented carefully.

When your child has reached a level of behavior that you're satisfied with (and this might not be perfect behavior, but only behavior that is within tolerable limits), then you begin to look for a way to fade out the tangible reinforcers. Go to the store and buy a package of stickers that are slightly larger than the ones you have been using. Substitute the larger stickers for the smaller ones, but give him the larger sticker only at the end of the entire half hour. In this way you are giving a reinforcer less frequently, you are giving a slightly larger reward so the child does not feel cheated, and you are meeting our guiding principles of switching over to a partial reinforcement schedule to ensure behavior that will be more resistant to extinction.

If you follow these procedures, you will find that after another week or so, you can begin to give your child the sticker every other day and put him on an even lower percentage of reinforcement. After another week or two nontangible rewards, the praise we spoke of, should be sufficient to maintain the behavior. At any time that the objectionable behavior starts to increase in frequency and there is a decrease in positive behavior, do not hesitate but go back immediately to an earlier step of this behavior change process and institute a more consistent, more tangible reward at whatever stage is necessary.

You might ask at this point whether these elaborate procedures are worthwhile. Clearly all of this requires a commitment and an effort on your part that has to be more than just a casual one. Is the payoff in the change of a child's behavior worth the effort required? We think it certainly is. There are several reasons for this conclusion. First, you will find that if you enable your child to control his behavior in one set of circumstances, there will be a slight positive effect in other areas as well, so you get a larger payoff than you might think at first.

Another important reason for instituting procedures like this is that you prove to yourself that your child's behavior is under your control, at least to some extent, and it reduces some of the frustration and chaos in your own life. You don't feel so helpless any longer and that creates a better mood for the entire family. It might even make you tolerate other disruptive behavior a little bit better. Perhaps most important of all is that it gives your child an opportunity to control his own behavior to some extent, and this should not only be a source of pride and satisfaction to him, but should also reduce some of his anxiety as he begins to see that his behavior is not as bad or out of control as he might have feared it was.

Methods of Decreasing (Extinguishing) Undesirable Behavior

Increasing desirable behavior and decreasing undesirable behavior usually go together. However, at times the undesirable behavior is so disruptive that parents do not have the luxury of trying to build up more positive behavior, so you have to stress eliminating the objectionable behavior. For example, if a child is so very disruptive at the dinner table or has temper tantrums of such severity that they create a great deal of tension for everyone else, these behaviors should be the focus for extinction procedures.

In earlier sections of this chapter we have discussed principles of learning (such as reinforcement schedules) which guide our extinction management program. With that background we can go immediately to specific examples, but we will continue to discuss the underlying principles as we go along for emphasis.

Consider the need to eliminate violent temper tantrums in a five-year-old child. The exact cause or causes of the temper tantrums need not concern us, but it is worth noting that children learn to have temper tantrums the same way they learn any other behavior: because it gets them something. So our first task is to identify what is rewarding or reinforcing the child when he has a temper tantrum. Reinforcers vary from child to child and family to family, but usually they are quite similar. There are two general reinforcers that keep temper tantrums going. The first is that it enables the child to get what he wants. Temper tantrums can be terrifying. Even the most experienced and capable parents, in the face of tantrum rages that go on for hours, begin to lose confidence in their judgment and common sense. Perhaps their child is ill, they think. Maybe he is having a seizure or some sort of fit. Is it possible that if you let him cry and go on like this for hours, he might have trouble breathing or choke and hurt himself? Parents become frightened that a child may get so out of control that "his mind might snap." Children can and do hold their breath till they turn blue and pass out. These temper tantrums cannot be taken lightly.

There is some common-sense wisdom that most parents have heard. Temper tantrums should be ignored. This is mighty fine advice to give to people and very easy to give, but much more difficult to put into operation when it is your child who is lying on the floor banging his head against the side of a dresser or table and seems completely out of control. Given the violence and bewildering behavior that children incorporate into their temper tantrums, it is not surprising that it is a very effective means to get their parents finally to give in and give them what they want.

The second major reinforcer for tantrum behavior is simply attention. A child can quite literally capture the full attention of every other human being within listening range with a loud, violent, temper tantrum. Even if the child fails to secure the toy or privilege he initially wanted, he can successfully immobilize the household and direct all of the family's attention to him. In this way he can, in effect, say, "You may not give me what I want, but in return I can make your life so miserable that you'll think carefully about it next time when you know I'm going to have another one of these temper tantrums."

There may be other reinforcers and any planned extinction program for your child must include a careful analysis of his behavior, the situation that provoked the temper tantrums, and how you, as parents, have responded. Looking carefully at all of these factors should give you considerable insight into what it is that is maintaining the tantrums. Nonetheless, the procedures for dealing with the behavior, once we understand it, are straightforward. We must look for ways to deprive the child of reinforcement.

As we mentioned much earlier in our example about the two children who used calling for a drink of water as a way of delaying bedtime, if you are considering beginning to extinguish your child's tantrum, do not even start unless you are thoroughly committed to seeing it through to the end. You should be aware that in the early stages of your attempt to regain control of your child's behavior, you may actually cause temper tantrums that are more frequent and even more violent in nature than those you have already seen. This should not alarm you. When faced with circumstances or people who try to get us to stop a well-established habit, any one of us will usually push a little harder, even double or triple our effort in order to continue to get our way. That is probably what is going to happen with your child. But if you know it in advance and understand the significance of the behavior, you will be more able to plan your actions and see it through to a satisfactory conclusion.

We should add a few more words about ignoring temper tantrums. Ignoring a temper tantrum is a good idea. The only problem is that it is difficult to do and does not work as well in actual practice as we would like. The theory is fine. Theoretically, by ignoring a temper tantrum, you deprive the child of reinforcers. You give him neither what he wants nor the attention he seems to be seeking. However, even very young children know that if they are lying on the living room rug kicking, screaming, and threatening to smash lamps and tear up furniture, you can hear them in the kitchen and be affected by their behavior. Furthermore, in the face of well-established tantrum habits, it is best to look for alternative ways of dealing with the tantrums that will allow parents a bit more peace of mind. Going into another room and pretending that you are not concerned about your child's screaming and threats to dismantle portions of the house rarely works out well.

The most effective means of extinguishing a temper tantrum is to isolate the child, preferably in his own bedroom. There are practical factors that might make this difficult and we will discuss them further on, but here we will outline what steps to take. First, explain to your child one more time that there are some new rules in the house. Point out that his tantrums are disruptive and they upset everyone, including the child himself, so from now on there are new rules. Any time he begins to fuss, you will ask him to go to his room and stay there until he has settled down on his own. Then he can come out and rejoin the family or go back to whatever activity he was engaged in.

Of course, by itself this explanation is not going to make a bit of difference in your child's behavior. We only suggest you do it because it is a clear signal that things are going to be different than they have been in the past, and you owe him an explanation about what is going to happen. From this point on, action is more important than talk. You know best whether your child understands the rules. Most children of age two can understand a rule such as you have just read. It does not gain any more force from being explained a second time or a 50th or 100th time. Too often, parents either try to reason with their children or explain the importance of rules and their consequences at times of greatest emotional turmoil. Consider your own experiences as an adult. In the midst of an argument, how receptive are you to someone else's heated explanation of why you are wrong and why you ought to change your behavior? Perhaps later in the day or on the following day, when you have calmed down, you might be receptive to the same arguments you would not listen to at all when you were angry or upset. The same applies to managing your child. If you want to explain things to him, do so later on, not at the time you're implementing the isolation procedures. Let your actions speak for you.

We think it's important to tell a child that he has to stay in his room only long enough to get his behavior under control, even if this means he marches in screaming and hollering and does an immediate about-face and walks back out. Realistically, this advice won't work very well with a child in the early stages of this procedure, and we will discuss that in more detail in a moment, but the emphasis on a child gaining control of his *own* behavior is what this entire exercise is all about. It is far more effective to emphasize his control of his behavior rather than your control of his behavior as a parent. Our goal is to get you out of the business of saying how long he should spend in his room. It may turn out that your child is incapable of gaining this control over his own impulses, but at least try.

The Early Stages. Be certain you've explained to your child what objectionable behavior is under consideration. It will not do to tell him that you are going to put him in his room when he's "bad." You will get nowhere if you tell him that you want him to "behave himself." Remember to make your descriptions of the behavior as objective as possible. Let him know that raising his voice above a certain level, hitting his sister, throwing food at the kitchen table, using offensive language are the behaviors you find objectionable. But keep in mind we are working to change behavior, not attitudes or feelings. And behavior can be, must be, clearly described.

To return to our example, immediately, the next time the tantrum begins, send the child to his room. If he refuses to go, pick him up and carry him there, place him in his room, turn around, close the door and walk out. Don't explain anything. Don't wait for the behavior to escalate into a major tantrum. Like most parents, you have probably developed a sixth sense, sensitively trying to read those early protests and preliminary threats to see whether this episode can be safely ignored or if it is going to turn out to be a typical temper tantrum or even one of the big ones. Forget those distinctions for the time being. Move swiftly. At the first sign of what looks like it could be the sort of behavior you want to extinguish, isolate the child in his room.

Now what? If your child is like most others, he won't stay there. He will probably be 3 feet behind you, still screaming and fussing, as you walk out of his room. Or he may stay in his room for a few minutes and even settle down, only to come out and resume the same disruptive behavior a few minutes later. Follow through. Do it again. Take him back to his room.

How long do you keep doing this? As long as necessary. If your child refuses to stay in his room, lock the door. If the door has no lock, go to a hardware store, get a small hook and eye, and latch the door from the outside. Leave the light on, assure the child in a calm, quiet way that you will be outside, and he can come out as soon as he settles down. The lock upsets many children. Reassure him calmly, but only once, that you will stop using the lock as soon as he gets sufficient control over his own behavior so that he stays in his room with it unlatched. If your child is having a tantrum protesting the lock loudly, it may seem that he does not hear your reassurance. Say it only once. Do not argue with him. Save your logical approach for a time when you are both calm. The use of the lock is only temporary and rarely necessary for more than a few days. After your child has settled down, remind him again, but only once, that you will use the lock only as long as he refuses to remain behind in his room.

These procedures should be sufficient for most tantrums. However, a few children will carry on their behavior to such an extent that new questions are raised. For example, how long do you allow a child to scream and kick in a violent rage in his room? The answer is simple: until he settles down. In some instances this can be four, five, or even six or eight hours. That is unusual, and if you hang on the first time for eight hours, you will probably never have to do it again. But it does happen.

Another question that comes up is, "What do we do if he starts destroying things in his room?" You know your child. It might be a good idea to remove most things from your child's room during the time in which you are trying to get these temper tantrums under control. It probably will be for no more than two weeks or so. You might want to put his dresser out in the hall and remove items from any shelves on the wall and possibly even clean out his closet. Alternatively, leave everything in his room and let him make as big a mess as he wants and don't clean it up. In a couple of days or weeks when the behavior is under control, have the child straighten up for himself—with your assistance.

Some children become so agitated that we fear for their safety. We have to recognize that a child can, in a rage, jump off his bed and bang his head against the corner of a dresser, or otherwise hurt himself. Windows can be broken. Light fixtures can be shattered. By now you are probably shaking your head and saying, "Not me. I'm not putting him or the family through that." You can also see why we warned you so thoroughly that you should not make a commitment to these procedures unless you're prepared to follow it through to the end. Perhaps furniture should be removed from the child's room. It may be, depending on your child, that it would be safest to leave only a mattress in his room. Many parents stand outside a child's door listening to the quiet that descends after hours of vigorous, violent protest, wondering fearfully what has become of their child. Has he hurt himself? Has he stopped breathing? Is he even still in there? You might find it helpful to drill a small observation hole through the door so you can inobtrusively peek into his room to reassure yourself he is safe. Drilling an observation hole in the door and fastening extra locks to the outside may destroy the door. Only you can decide whether the cost of a new door is worth paying for better control over your child's tantrum behavior.

Children do not hurt themselves physically or mentally from temper tantrums. However, if your child's behavior is especially difficult to control, such as we have described in the last few pages, it would be best for your child and for your own peace of mind if such a behavior management program was under the direction of either your family doctor or a psychologist or psychiatrist. These doctors can reassure you about your child's response to your strict management, give you guidance and support when your confidence flags, and deal with any feelings of anger or hostility this creates in your child. Temporarily, your child might become very angry with you. Nonetheless, that sort of anger can be managed relatively easily and is far less destructive than the long-term feelings of hostility, alienation, and rejection that arise in families if the temper tantrum behavior is allowed to persist.

It is not easy to listen to your child tell you he hates you and, in many ways, it is even more frightening when, in your own mind, you begin to think, I hate you too. These are normal responses to this kind of situation, but everyone will feel better if you have a chance to talk them over with a professional person.

The Middle Stage. You should be able to see substantial change in both the frequency and intensity of the tantrums within a few days. You'll know when you are on the right track. In the middle stage of management you should be able to begin to place more responsibility on your child. The lock on the door should no longer be necessary. He should be going to his room on his own when you send him. Guard again premature feelings of success. You must remain very consistent. Continue to intervene quickly. Do not allow second chances. Do not tie yourself up with lengthy explanations. It is very tempting to tell your child that by now you think he should understand all of the rules and you cannot understand why he does not seem to be following along when you first tell him to go to his room. If you take the time to have that discussion with him, you are undermining your own consistency and management program. If he has been going to his room regularly when you instruct him to do so and one time hesitates, take him gently but firmly by the hand and move him along. If he comes out of his room too quickly and begins the same argument over again, you might have to lock him in another time or two.

Overall, continue at calm times to place an emphasis on his own control of his own behavior. At this point you might also introduce a positive reinforcement program for hours or days when he has no tantrum. The same procedures we have described earlier can be applied by the hour, the half-day, or the day for the child who is now going for longer and longer periods of time without temper tantrums.

The Final Stage. There are only a very few rules we can offer with absolute, 100 percent, ironclad certainty. One such rule is this: if your child is tantrum-free for several weeks, you believe you have the problem completely in hand, and you relax your vigilance, you can be assured that the temper tantrums will come right back, probably as strong as ever. Although it will be needed less often, you still must remain ready to go back to the strictest application of the procedures already discussed at any time the temper tantrums seem to reappear. Your child might very well try it again. Don't give the behavior a chance to become re-established.

4 Educational Planning and Management

Children with Attention Deficit Disorder often have problems in school. Many of the same difficulties they have at home also interfere in the classroom and on the playground. They may also have trouble with the schoolwork itself. By high school approximately 30 percent of students with ADD have repeated a grade, and about 60 percent are from one to two years behind the achievement level we would expect if they did not have a learning problem. There are many reasons for these problems, ranging from the inability to concentrate on lessons to far more complex reasons, including many of the different learning characteristics that we have already discussed. In addition, many children with ADD have *learning disabilities*. For example, visual-perception problems are common, and there is some evidence that visual memory is not quite as good in children with ADD as in their peers. Visual memory refers to the ability to see something and remember what it looks like. This skill is important in the early stages of learning to read.

Still unanswered is the question of whether children with ADD have some additional special disability in these areas, or if their problem in visual memory or other aspects of learning can be explained entirely in terms of poor attention span, impulsivity, and heightened distractibility. The best research to date seems to suggest that, for the majority of youngsters with ADD, problems paying attention are the primary handicap in the classroom. However, for a smaller but significant number of children with ADD, there are additional learning disabilities as well that remain even after the attentional problems have been dealt with.

Learning Disabilities and the Child with ADD

A full discussion of learning disabilities is beyond the scope of this book, but some background will be useful. About 10 percent of all children, no matter what is done in the classroom, simply do not learn as well as would be expected based on their intellectual abilities. As we have already noted, there is an even higher incidence of learning problems among youngsters with ADD and/or hyperactivity than among other groups. Children with learning disabilities are not all the same. *Learning disability* isn't really a medical or psychological diagnosis; it is only a description of a problem. Many different handicaps seem to cause learning disabilities.

A psychiatric or psychological diagnosis of learning disability may differ in some details from the definition of learning disability used in your child's school. This is because each state department of education establishes the criteria for classifying a child as learning disabled in that state. Nonetheless, there is considerable agreement and uniformity, and most state education departments' definitions of learning disability are based on national standards and include certain general features.

A learning disability generally means a disorder in one or more of the basic psychological processes involved in understanding or in using language, spoken or written, which may show up as an imperfect ability to listen, think, speak, read, write, spell, or do mathematical calculations. The term *learning disability* generally includes such conditions as perceptual handicaps, brain injury, minimal brain dysfunction, dyslexia, and developmental aphasia. The term generally does not include children who have learning problems which are primarily the result of visual, hearing, or motor handicaps, of mental retardation, of severe psychological disturbance, or of cultural or economic disadvantage.

When a child has had a learning experience and instruction that is appropriate to his age and ability level but does not achieve commensurate with his age and ability level in one or more of the areas listed below, schools generally determine the child has a learning disability and classify him as learning disabled. The areas of problem achievement are expression, listening comprehension, written expression, basic reading skills, reading comprehension, mathematics calculation, and mathematic reasoning. A bit further on, we will discuss the process by which school personnel typically make the evaluation that leads to a decision about whether or not a child is learning disabled.

As we noted above, many children with learning problems are children with attention problems. Other difficulties found include visual-motor coordination problems, perceptual problems, visual and auditory memory problems, and frequently, clumsiness. The last may interfere with the youngster's penmanship and create a lot of frustration as teachers become increasingly demanding as the years go on for better penmanship. Perceptual problems often show up as an inability to discriminate right from left and confusion of "b" with "d" or "p" with "q." Children with perceptual problems may write or copy figures and letters backward or upside down. Confusion of right and left is a normal part of development for five-year-old and many six-year-old children, but problems such as these become of concern to educators when they persist beyond this age.

Special Education Procedures

Every school district has guidelines for step-by-step procedures that allow for a determination of whether or not a child has a learning disability. In all cases, the determination of a disability will be based on a comprehensive evaluation by a multi-disciplinary evaluation team. The members of this team may differ from state to state and school district to school district, but in all cases the membership of this multi-disciplinary team is spelled out and steps by which the diagnosis and evaluations are undertaken are written down. You can get this information from any education department or special education department.

The evaluation team always includes some contribution by a child's regular teacher. If for some reason the child is not in school at the time the determination of disability is made, a regular classroom teacher qualified to teach a child of his or her age is usually included to provide some information. In addition, the multi-disciplinary evaluation team usually includes at least one person qualified to conduct individual diagnostic examinations of children, such as a school psychologist, a teacher of students who are speech- and language-impaired, or some other specialist. In addition, school social workers frequently assist in gathering information. In the case of older children, a school counselor, administrator, and a variety of classroom teachers may make a contribution.

When teachers suspect a child has some learning impairment, permission from parents is usually sought to allow members of this specialized multi-disciplinary team to undertake the evaluation. After completing their testing and evaluation, the members of this team meet with parents (a procedure that is required by law in all states), and a specialized instructional plan, often called an Individualized Education Plan (IEP) is formulated. The plan includes contributions from all of the people who are familiar with the child, as well as the parents, and, in the case of older children, often the contribution of the child himself. If there is agreement between home and school, the program is implemented with appropriate follow-up and evaluation to determine how successful the program has been. There are subsequent meetings of the planning committee whenever necessary, and always whenever any change in the program is made. If parents and school personnel cannot agree on what should be done, every state provides, in law, guidelines that describe the rights parents have to make appeals and to have hearings before appropriate educational and legal agencies in order to present their case for their child's needs.

To the best of our knowledge, in no state is a child eligible for special education help solely because of ADD. The majority of children with ADD, when they are certified as special education students, are classified as either learning disabled or emotionally disturbed. In many cases the diagnosis of learning disability or emotional disturbance is in error. As we noted earlier, the symptoms of Attention Deficit Disorder are often misunderstood or misinterpreted. For some children, this error is a fortunate one because it means the child will get special help that would otherwise be denied. For others, failure to recognize the Attention Deficit Disorder and its relationship to learning and behavior problems creates additional hardship for the child.

One of the most difficult problems arises in those cases where the child's learning or behavior is affected by ADD, but not severely enough to allow him to be assigned to special education. Unfortunately, as time goes by and the child gets older, the learning handicap and behavioral problems usually become more severe. By the time a child does meet the criteria for placement in a special education program, a lot of time has been wasted, and the child's psychological problems have become worse.

Two Cases of Misdiagnosis

Many children with ADD, of course, do have learning disabilities, and many have emotional disturbances. It is often difficult to determine the precise nature of the relationships between learning and emotional problems and ADD. A child may do poorly in school because he is anxious or because of Attention Deficit Disorder. Similarly, a child with a learning disability, who finds schoolwork especially difficult, may become nervous and seem inattentive or disinterested in the work. It may be hard to sort it all out and decide what came first and what caused what.

Many children with Attention Deficit Disorder require special help that can be obtained only in a special education class. Sometimes ADD is misdiagnosed and the child is placed in a special class when that may not be necessary. Other times, a child has Attention Deficit Disorder and needs special class placement but is not eligible according to strict school regulations. Many youngsters with ADD do not require anything more than some modest adjustments in their school program and expectations; others require more extensive care. It depends on the individual case.

Following are two case studies describing common errors in diagnosis and conceptualization of school-related problems of children with ADD.

Benjamin Collins

Benjamin Collins seemed to develop normally until he began kindergarten. Toward the end of the year Ben's teacher told his parents he was immature and recommended that he repeat the grade. She regarded him as immature because of his inability to settle down and follow instructions. She noted that he was responsive to her efforts at discipline and did his work properly when she sat with him or stood over him, but when left alone he was mildly disruptive and could not seem to finish anything.

After his second year in kindergarten, Ben's teacher still had reservations about his behavior but felt he was ready for first grade. She knew he was a bright boy, and he seemed eager to learn. She noted on his report card that he had made a great deal of progress through the year, but continual effort in the area of self-control and working independently would be required if he was to be successful.

Ben did not do as well in first grade as might be expected, based on his apparent level of intelligence, but he had a teacher his parents regarded as strict but flexible, and with some extra help, by the end of first grade everyone agreed that he could safely be promoted.

Three months into second grade, toward the end of November, Ben's teacher asked his parents to come to school for a conference. Ben was not doing the work. The teacher told Mr. and Mrs. Collins that he "could do it if he wanted to." She described him as immature and emotionally needy. He required a great deal of her attention. She suggested a psychological evaluation, because she thought Benjamin might be psychologically disturbed.

Mr. and Mrs. Collins were upset, of course. They regarded themselves as capable parents, but after 3½ years of frustration with Benjamin's behavior in school, they no longer felt as confident as they once did. They were especially troubled by the suggestion that their son demanded a great deal of attention. They questioned his teacher carefully, and it seemed the only evidence she could muster in support of this idea was the fact that when she gave Benjamin attention by working with him alone, he did satisfactorily. Without the attention he did poorly. On the basis of that, she concluded he must either need attention or feel very insecure.

It was the matter of Benjamin's security that was so troubling to his parents. If Benjamin was insecure, it could only mean that he did not feel loved. That meant they were failing as parents.

There was further consultation with specialists within the school and Benjamin's pediatrician. The school social worker and psychologist made a recommendation that Ben be classified as emotionally disturbed and placed in a special education class.

After 3½ years in school, Ben had been labeled immature, insecure, possessing a bad attitude toward school, lacking motivation, possibly learning disabled, and psychologically disturbed.

They were all wrong!

Ben had Attention Deficit Disorder. Fortunately, the teacher of the class for emotionally disturbed children into which Ben was placed recognized the zebra's hoofbeats and urged Mr. and Mrs. Collins to have Benjamin evaluated at a clinic with a professional staff knowledgeable about

ADD. Unfortunately, after years of frustration and failure, Benjamin did have the beginnings of some psychological problems that required additional psychological treatment for about six months. However, after being treated with medication, he returned to a regular classroom and, following another year of remedial help to catch up, was able to do satisfactorily in a regular class where his achievement and behavior were no longer of any concern.

Benjamin was one of the lucky ones. Although he had to wait until he was nine years old before an alert teacher recognized the symptoms of ADD, the problem was diagnosed early enough so that something could be done. In addition, although Benjamin had developed some psychological problems and was behind in his schoolwork, these deficiencies were mild enough so that they were treatable and resolved within a short period of time. Unfortunately, the frustrating four years that Benjamin spent in school with repeated failure, misguided efforts to help on the part of his teachers, and the continually building frustration and discouragement leading to psychological problems, goes on and on for other children. Many children, as they get older, become more disillusioned with school, and the likelihood of their dropping out and developing more serious psychological problems is high.

In the next case study you will see how a decision to certify a nine-year-old boy as eligible for special education, based on the mistaken notion that he had a learning disability, led to a gratifying improvement in his school performance. The problem that resulted from the misdiagnosis did not arise until it was time to return the student to a regular education program.

Matthew Richardson

Matthew Richardson was nine years old when he first came to the attention of the school psychologist. He had repeated first grade. By the middle of third grade his teacher discussed his progress with Mr. and Mrs. Richardson, and they decided to have the school psychologist test Matt. Despite the best efforts of all of Matthew's teachers, his reading level remained at a mid- to late-first-grade level. His arithmetic achievement was somewhat better, but that, too, lagged at least a year behind what would be expected, based on his current grade placement.

In contrast to Benjamin Collins, despite poor school achievement, Matthew was a boy with a pleasant disposition and a cheerful, outgoing manner. He was troubled by the poor quality of his schoolwork, but it did not seem to affect his behavior in other areas of his life.

The school psychologist administered the Wechsler Intelligence Scale for Children to Matthew. He scored considerably above average in most areas of the test with a Full Scale IQ of 114. Standardized achievement test results were consistent with the reports of the teacher. The psychologist's tests showed Matthew to be reading at about the end of the first-grade level and doing arithmetic at the latter part of the second-grade level. History, the interview, and results of personality tests revealed no signs of significant psychological disturbance, although the psychologist's report did say that Matthew was somewhat immature. That judgment appeared to be based on the fact that Matthew seemed somewhat irresponsible and could not follow through on instructions. At times, he seemed to be more interested in playing than working.

The psychologist was able to rule out low intelligence and psychological disturbance as causes of Matthew's learning problem. It remained to be determined whether Matthew had a learning disability. As we noted earlier, there is considerable ambiguity in the definitions of learning disabilities, and there appear to be many types. For Matthew, the school psychologist included several tests of visual perception, visual motor coordination, and perceptual integration in the test battery.

Matthew did poorly on several perceptual motor tests, especially the Bender Visual Motor Gestalt Test and the Beery Developmental Test of Visual Motor Integration. Both of these tests require a child to copy a variety of geometric shapes and designs. Matthew's reproductions were clumsy, poorly defined, and badly organized on the page.

A psychological or medical diagnosis is made on the basis of the absence of certain signs and symptoms and the presence of others. In Matthew's case the absence of any signs of any psychological disturbance or low intelligence allowed those possibilities to be ruled out. The presence of a perceptual problem, taken together with Matthew's failure to benefit from regular classroom instruction for so many years, and his poor achievement when considered on the basis of what we would expect considering how smart he was, led to a diagnosis of learning disability.

A school committee consisting of Matthew's teacher and the school psychologist, learning disability consultant, counselor, and principal met with Mr. and Mrs. Richardson and recommended that Matthew be certified as learning disabled and placed in a special education class, where he would get extensive and intensive individual help from a specially trained teacher. Mr. and Mrs. Richardson were grateful for the opportunity to finally do something for their son and readily agreed. Matthew was also relieved and happy with the idea of getting some help for a problem that had frustrated him for so long.

Shortly after Matthew was placed in the special education program, Mrs. Richardson discussed the matter with Matthew's pediatrician. He agreed that the plan seemed sensible but suggested that Matthew be evaluated by a child psychologist at a nearby clinic for a second opinion. The child psychologist reviewed the test results obtained by the school psychologist, and his attention was drawn to the reports of immature behavior, especially Matthew's disorganization, his occasional silliness, and descriptions of how he would rather play than work. He could hear the hoofbeats pounding in the distance. Horses, he wondered, or possibly zebras?

At an appointment with Matthew's parents, the psychologist carefully, in great detail, reviewed Matthew's behavior and development. He also asked the parents and Matthew's teachers to fill out several behavior rating scales including the Connors. In addition, the psychologist reviewed Matthew's school records including his report cards, school papers that his mother kept in a folder at home, and anecdotal materials maintained by the school in Matthew's permanent record. The words "short attention span" and "problems with self-control" appeared frequently. Nonetheless, these problems were usually interpreted by Matthew's teachers as reflections of immaturity, rather than as signals that something else might be wrong.

Based on this careful appraisal of Matthew's history, a diagnosis of ADD without Hyperactivity was made. It was recognized that Matthew's Attention Deficit Disorder was of only moderate severity and that neither his short attention span nor his problems with impulse control seemed to create any behavioral disturbance, other than his inability to complete his schoolwork. Poor schoolwork usually causes concern, but the child who also has a behavior problem is more likely to come to the attention of professionals and be diagnosed earlier. In Matthew's case, because his Attention Deficit Disorder was expressed as only a learning problem, the significance of the behaviors underlying the learning problem was not recognized.

About six weeks after Matthew began in the special education program he was placed on Ritalin.

Matthew did very well in special education. He seemed to enjoy it, he appeared motivated, and his progress was gratifying. He completed the third grade in a self-contained special education classroom and began fourth grade spending half the day in special education and half the day in regular classroom programs.

At the end of the fourth grade, the treatment plan was to begin to wean him even further from special education, so in fifth grade he spent two periods a day in the special classroom with a teacher he had now had for three years, and who knew him well, and the rest of the day in a regular fifth grade. The school planning committee met with Mr. and Mrs. Richardson in April of Matthew's fifth-grade year and heard reports from his general education and special education teachers that were very positive. Matthew reportedly was achieving at grade level and all present at the meeting were happy to endorse the decision to return Matthew to a regular education program full time for the sixth grade.

It was a decision made in ignorance and it was a disaster!

In early November Matthew's counselor and one of his sixth-grade teachers asked for a meeting with Mr. and Mrs. Richardson. The quality of Matthew's schoolwork had deteriorated markedly, and he had become increasingly belligerent and uncooperative. This came as a surprise to Matthew's parents, because he showed no such behavior at home and had told them that he was doing well. They were anticipating an excellent first report card.

Mr. and Mrs. Richardson agreed to work closely with the teachers and counselor to monitor Matthew's behavior and homework assignments. They all agreed they would meet again shortly after the first of the year to evaluate Matthew's status.

By mid-January Matthew's work had deteriorated further, and his angry attitude about schoolwork spilled over at home. His parents were now arguing with him about incomplete assignments, and it was a rare evening in the Richardson household when there wasn't at least one angry outburst, leading to hurt feelings and tears. Toward the end of the month he began to refuse to take his medicine.

What had happened? What went wrong? Matthew seemed to have overcome his learning disability. He was still taking Ritalin. But he had gone from satisfactory achievement and a good disposition to failing work and a dreadful attitude.

The answer to the question of what went wrong lies in a better understanding of why Matthew had learning problems in the first place. This boy, who was now 12 years old, had been diagnosed as learning disabled when he was 9. Most of the decisions that had been made about his educational programming were based on the image of him as learning disabled. But Matthew never had a learning disability. At first, the error in diagnosis actually helped him because it enabled him to get special education help that compensated to some extent for his ADD. However, it was that same error in diagnosis that then led to the ill-fated decision to remove Matthew from special education and put him into a general education program full time.

Matthew had done well in special education, not because he had a learning disability and was being taught by a learning disabilities teacher, but because he had Attention Deficit Disorder and responded well to the high degree of structure and support inherent in the LD special education classroom. He did so well for all of those years, in part, because he benefited from the effect of the medicine, but even more importantly, because the special program he was in helped compensate for the difficulties he had with attention span, distractibility, and disorganization.

This is where an accurate understanding of the problem is crucial. The special education program worked, but not for the reasons everyone thought it did. Matthew's learning disability was not being cured because he did not have a learning disability in the first place. So a decision to return him to the regular classroom, based on the idea that his learning disability had been somehow remediated, was completely off track. As soon as the extra support (and remember Matthew only needed it for two periods a day) was taken from him in sixth grade, Matthew fell flat on his face.

Unfortunately, it was not a simple matter to rectify the error and put Matthew back into special education. By the time the full impact of the unfortunate decision was understood, it was March of Matthew's sixth-grade year, and he had had six months to get angry, frustrated, and discouraged about himself. He was no longer 9 years old—he was almost 13, with all of the difficulties that early adolescence brings. He was threatened and frightened by the poor quality of his schoolwork, and his fear made him more angry. He vigorously resisted the suggestion that he return to the special education class for several hours a day, insisting that he did not need any help. He said he could do the work if he wanted to; he just didn't want to. No amount of logic or reasonable discussion by anyone would persuade him otherwise. He stopped taking all medicine.

Ultimately, the story of Matthew Richardson has a positive ending. Matthew was able to develop a good relationship with the clinical psychologist who originally examined him and who provided supportive psychological counseling. He was able to help Matthew understand the causes of his learning difficulties, as well as his bad feelings about himself. By September of the following year Matthew was willing to begin taking his medicine again and accept two periods a day in the special education resource room. Over the next several years, that provided sufficient support and extra help for Matthew so he was able to get his schoolwork back on track, and although he never obtained grades that might be expected based on his IQ level, he passed all of his courses and is doing satisfactorily in tenth grade at the time of this writing.

The erroneous diagnosis of learning disability reflects errors that occur every day. The definition of a learning disability requires that the learning problem not be caused by limited intelligence, faulty instruction, psychological disturbance, or social factors, such as a severely disrupted family. Those are the negatives that have to be ruled out. The positive findings that allow certification as learning disabled include a variety of language and language processing disabilities and the perceptual problem that Matthew was thought to display. So in essence, although there was solid evidence in Matthew's case to rule out other causes of learning problems, the only positive factor to support a diagnosis of learning disability was his poor performance on the perceptual tests. About half of all children labeled learning disabled have been so classified on the basis of perceptual or perceptual motor problems.

Although given scant attention at the time because Matthew was doing so well in special education class, there were test records in his file that showed the diagnosis of perceptual problem had been in error. Approximately three weeks after Matthew began taking Ritalin he was retested on several of the tests that had been used as part of the school psychologist's initial test battery. Among those tests were the Bender Gestalt Test and the Beery Perceptual Development Test. In both cases Matthew was taking Ritalin at the time these tests were repeated. The quality of Matthew's performance was markedly improved over that of the initial testing. The improvement reflected gains far beyond what would be expected, based just on the fact that he had practiced these designs before. Results of this second administration of the perceptual tests showed no evidence of a perceptual problem.

Just to be certain, the psychologist tested Matthew again with the same tests several hours later in the day, when Matt's medicine had worn off. The quality of his performance was, not surprisingly, almost identical to that he displayed when first tested by the school psychologist. The poor quality of the drawings reflected not a perceptual problem, not a visual-motor integration problem, nor any other kind of coordination or perceptual problem, but rather that Matthew's distractibility and impulsivity lay at the root of poor test performance. While it is certainly true that poor performance on these tests is often indicative of a perceptual problem, poor quality work may reflect other things as well. In Matthew's case, his clumsy drawings were an expression of the symptoms of Attention Deficit Disorder. Listen carefully for the zebra's hoofbeats!

Managing the Child in School

Treatment of learning problems has to be based on an accurate assessment of the nature of the problem. Unfortunately, a lot of questionable remedial educational programs have been developed for children with learning problems. Many of them have been called perceptual-motor training programs. These run the gamut from eye-training exercises through extensive practice tracing and copying geometric figures to the presentation of stimuli via tactile and kinesthetic means, as well as auditory and visual. These sorts of practice exercises do not seem to do anything to help children learn to read. They are a waste of time for children with ADD who have learning problems. A joint statement prepared a number of years ago by the American Academy of Pediatrics, the American Academy of Ophthalmology and Otolaryngology, and the American Association of Ophthalmology stated: "No known scientific evidence supports claims for improving the academic abilities of learning disabled or dyslexic children with treatment based solely on visual training (or) neurologic organizational training (balance board, perceptual training)."

Children with ADD who have reading problems can be helped. There are a number of fairly sophisticated remedial programs that are effective. They are expensive in terms of time, however. It is vitally important that the temptation to look for shortcuts be avoided. Consideration must be given to the reading level of the child. Often, if a 10-year-old child has the reading skills of a first-grade student, teachers and parents are impatient and do not want to start remediation at the first-grade level. This is necessary, however. Impatience and reliance on shortcuts account for many of the failures of remedial reading programs.

This is particularly important with children with ADD, who require careful, meticulous attention to detail and organization, as we have discussed earlier. The best remedial reading program for most children with ADD who have learning problems is a rigorous emphasis on phonics, teaching reading with a great deal of overlearning at each level, and absolutely no progression to the next stage before a child has mastered each level of skills. The techniques whereby this is done are developed from the principles we have discussed above about how children with ADD learn.

Most children with Attention Deficit Disorder can be taught effectively in a regular classroom. Often they will need some supplemental or remedial help, but they can remain in a regular school program. If the problem is recognized early and treated thoroughly medically, psychologically, and educationally, achievement problems can usually be held to a minimum. When the primary ADD diagnosis is neglected and children are placed in special classes for students with other handicaps, children with ADD do receive some of the extra help they need, such as a higher degree of structure and organization which they cannot provide themselves, and more individual instruction. So placement in these special classes is of some benefit. The negative side of the issue, however, is that seeing a child respond somewhat positively in one of these special education classes is often taken to confirm the erroneous diagnosis that led to his placement there in the first place. Thus, as in Matt's case, appropriate medical and psychological care is delayed even longer, and the child is denied the chance to be educated in a regular school classroom.

School is a source of much frustration for children with ADD (and for their teachers, too). But an understanding of ADD helps everyone. Share this book with your child's teacher. Everyone working with a child with Attention Deficit Disorder must remember that the problems he has in the classroom and in social relationships at school are of a chronic nature. This means they will not be cured or totally eliminated. Everyone must learn to deal with the fact that there is going to be a higher level of disruption in the classroom and in the lives of people who are with youngsters with ADD. This does not mean they should be allowed to run free or intrude upon other people. It does not mean that the school or family must compromise in terms of expectations and values for the child. But it does mean a more relaxed, more accepting, more understanding approach to a lot of his learning and behavioral characteristics.

Far too many children with ADD carry home from school every day exercise books and worksheets with abusive, critical, insensitive comments from teachers. There has never been a child with ADD who has been helped by a teacher scrawling across the top of a clumsily done arithmetic worksheet with 9 out of 10 problems wrong, the comment "John is going to have to improve his attitude and his work habits or he'll find himself in summer school." Labeling children as "immature," "lazy," or "attention-seeking," without considering what might underlie the behavior, is a main cause of the poor opinion many youngsters with ADD and learning disabilities have about themselves. Faced with this sort of criticism and feeling helpless about making the work any better, a child with ADD has little choice. Two avenues are open to him. In order to protect what little, fragile self-esteem he has remaining, he may begin to try to convince himself that school is unimportant and that the people who have high achievement expectations for him are either irrelevant to what is important in his life, or else his enemies in some way, and he rejects the idea that school is of any value at all to him. Many of these children then try to bolster their fragile sense of self-esteem by looking for status in other ways. Sadly, the things they often do to make themselves feel better, such as join delinquent gangs, commit acts of vandalism, begin using marijuana or smoking cigarettes or getting drunk, skip school, or perform other acts of rebellion, get them into further trouble. This, then, causes them to be rejected even more by the very people whose acceptance they so desperately hunger for. A vicious cycle is thus perpetuated. The other route that the disillusioned, discouraged youngster with ADD takes when he finds he cannot satisfy his parents and teachers is to withdraw, become apathetic, or become disinterested. He differs from the child who chooses the path of rebellion by letting you see more directly the feelings of hurt and discouragement and often anxiety. But he is no better off simply because he shows his feelings more openly, and the same downward spiral continues until, it is to be hoped, it is interrupted by appropriate medical, psychological, and educational management.

A report of research by psychologists at the University of California offers dramatic evidence of the interaction between the behavior of children with ADD and their teachers. The researchers studied the behavior of teachers toward a group of hyperactive children, one-half of whom received Ritalin and one-half a placebo. The teachers did not know which children received which type of pill. Teachers' behavior toward the children with ADD on Ritalin changed markedly. They began to respond to them just as they did to other children. There was no change in their behavior toward the children receiving the placebo, however. With this latter group, the teachers were more intense and controlling. They gave more orders to these children, scolded them more often, spoke louder and more rapidly to them, and smiled at them less. Other researchers have demonstrated similar patterns in the parents of children with ADD. This is all evidence of many complex factors that have to be considered in evaluating and treating the child with ADD. There is rarely a single cause for behavior. For each of us, even the youngest child, life is very complex. Constant reminders to ourselves of this complexity is essential if we are to be most helpful to our children with ADD.

Setting Goals

Helping a child with ADD learn to follow the rules, develop a sense of responsibility, and learn to control his own behavior requires careful attention to goal-setting. When setting standards for behavior for most children, it is often possible to get by with a general idea of what you would like done. You must be more specific and explicit with a child who has Attention Deficit Disorder. Recall our discussion in Chapter 3 of the learning characteristics of children with ADD. They must have clearly stated goals, and you must provide contingent reinforcement.

The teacher who wants a child to take a book home in order to complete an assignment may regard that as a single goal, but such an expectation is really a combination of goals. One is the goal that the book get to the child's home. Another goal often included, but not made explicit, is for the child to remember the book and accept the responsibility for taking it home himself. Now, if the goal is to get the book home, in his or her own mind, the teacher must be sure to separate that from the goal of having the child do it on his own. The latter goal may not be possible, and if the teacher fails to recognize that, he or she may not take the steps necessary to ensure the success of the first goal, simply getting the book home.

Therefore, the thoughtful teacher with carefully worked out goals will make an extra effort as the child leaves the classroom to be in a position to supervise and see to it that, when the student walks out the door, he is carrying his book. It may be necessary to go so far as to chase the child out the front door of the school to hand him his book. Another teacher may go to the extreme of stopping by the child's house on the way home to drop off the book if he left it at school. Of course, there are limits to how far any teacher should be expected to go in this regard. We carried this example to such an extreme point, however, to emphasize that, with children with ADD, our goals must be clear-cut and our commitment to them firmly based on our knowledge about ADD.

Once again, we are mindful of the fact that we must not encourage a child's dependency or manipulation. Many children would like to be relieved of the responsibility for remembering their books and supplies and be able to rely on the teacher to drop them off at their home. All children can easily learn bad habits, and it is possible, if we are not careful, to encourage dependency in the child with ADD to the point where he always looks to others to help compensate for his handicap. Nonetheless, despite the dangers, frustration, and extra work inherent in the approach to management of the child with ADD advocated here, we must never lose sight of the fact that this child has a significant handicap that requires that he be treated differently. Again, we are reminded that this child's inability to stay organized and keep his mind on carrying his book home at the end of the day does not reflect immaturity, a bad attitude, or irresponsibility. It is a symptom of a physical disorder and requires compensatory help in a manner no different than another child with a more obvious physical handicap would require.

Another common practice provides an excellent illustration of the importance of clear goal setting for children with ADD. A note sent home by the teacher is often a helpful means to assist a child to keep assignments in order, to keep track of homework and other projects due, and to provide a means for communication between teacher and parent. Parents are then in a good position to follow through and see to it that the homework is done. Completed work gives the child a feeling of success and accomplishment, rather than another experience of failure.

The frequency of notes from teacher to parent and back from parent to teacher should depend on the goal—what everyone expects to accomplish with the notes. If, for example, the goal is simply communication to keep the parent informed, then a note every week or two should be sufficient. If the goal is to obtain parental support for a particular project or assignment, such as a book report, or an effort requiring library research, then the note would be sent home only when these special needs arise.

On the other hand, the most common reason for using notes such as these is to ensure that the student keeps up his assignments, completes the homework, and turns it in. If this is the goal, it requires a daily note. Only a daily note will ensure that the work is done on a timely basis. We have seen many examples where a child brings home a note on Friday listing all incomplete assignments for the week. We cannot help but wonder what goal was held in mind for a once-a-week note system. Is the child expected to take two days to make up all of the work that he found impossible to do in five days? If that is the goal, it seems unrealistic. How can we possibly expect a child who cannot concentrate on his work long enough to complete it efficiently in five days, to be able to do the work in two?

It has been our experience that there is a strong punitive component, perhaps not explicit in the minds of parents and teachers but there, nonetheless, in cases where homework assignment notes are sent home once a week on Friday. It is as if someone is saying to the child, "Okay, if you don't want to do your work during the week, you can just sacrifice your weekend."

If we analyze such a statement in terms of the goal implied, it seems to say that the goal is not so much to help the child get the work done, but to punish him for not doing it. That is probably not what most parents and teachers intend, but it is the sort of thing that happens if careful attention is not given to formulating a clear idea of the goal and to developing a plan that leads you to that goal. Here we will limit our discussion to the issue of goal setting. In the circumstances we are dealing with in the present example, the goal is clearly to help the child complete as much of his schoolwork as possible.

If the goal is to help a child finish schoolwork, notes have to be sent every day. There has to be a clear-cut system worked out between school and home. This is the only way that we can realistically expect the job to get done. We will discuss a detailed plan for supervision of homework later in this chapter.

We are mindful that not all teachers, schools, or parents are willing or able to develop and maintain such a program. Many do it for a while and then become discouraged when the inevitable complications occur, and the program is either discarded or allowed to lapse. There are no halfway measures that will allow for halfway success. Not all children need such an elaborate program, but the teacher of a student who does or the parents of such a child must either provide for his needs or take into consideration their own reluctance to do so when they respond to his failure.

It is easy to lose sight of your goals and, because of anger and frustration with the child with ADD, allow your management techniques to become punitive. In the back of many people's minds is the ever recurring phrase, "She brought this on herself" to justify either hurtful punishment or allowing the child to fall into situations that are painful but need not have occurred.

For example, Sarah is a hyperactive 5½-year-old kindergarten student who was put in the corner for acting up during recess. Can you guess what the teacher's goal was? We do not know, but it was probably some vaguely formulated goal having to do with forcing Sarah to behave better. Now, if the teacher's goal was to frustrate and embarrass Sarah and to add to the peer-relation problems she had, then the strategy developed—putting her in the corner—worked well. The teacher knew Sarah was hyperactive and knew she was being treated with medication and psychological counseling. The teacher should have known that putting Sarah in the corner would have no effect at all on her behavior during recess. It would, if anything, make it worse.

To say, as Sarah's teacher did, that Sarah was given three chances and three warnings before she was put in the corner begs the issue of what the goals were. This treatment of Sarah is still cruel and ineffective punishment.

For Sarah, recess, gym class, lunchtime and other unstructured activities which allow her to be active are times fraught with peril. She becomes overexcited and finds it difficult to put restraints on her own behavior, and her normal hyperactive tendency to keep moving is exaggerated further. This means she requires greater supervision on the playground. It means that the teacher will have to develop greater tolerance for Sarah's inability to stand quietly in line waiting her turn and for her difficulty settling down to quiet activities after a period of excitement and physical activity. It does not mean the teacher must tolerate significant disruption of the class program or the activities of other children or allow the safety of others to be imperiled.

If Sarah cannot control her behavior with proper supervision and realistic expectations, it may be necessary to exclude her from a particular activity, in this case gym class. Excluding Sarah from gym would not be pleasant for her. It would be another failure. It would deprive her of an activity she enjoys. Nonetheless, it could be done in a positive, constructive way by giving her an alternative activity that carried with it a sense of pride and accomplishment. Even at 5½ years of age, Sarah could be helped to understand she has problems in unstructured situations, but that she was not being punished, humiliated, or rejected because of them. Rather, she was being protected from those problems and offered an alternative activity that she would enjoy.

This is not a perfect solution. It requires extra effort on the part of educational personnel and it cannot (and in fact, should not) be hidden from Sarah that this is a compromise solution in the face of a serious problem. Nonetheless, such a compromise is often necessary and would be consistent with our goals for a child such as Sarah. We will return to the subject of goal setting and non-punitive discipline in Chapter 5.

Lack of Motivation

Motivation to do well in school, especially in young children, is something many parents and teachers misunderstand. "If only we could motivate him" is a phrase heard so often it would lead us to think lack of motivation or disinterest in school is the primary problem most teachers face.

The apparent lack of motivation, like so many symptoms and behaviors already discussed, is often misleading. Think about it for a moment. The young child who comes to kindergarten or first grade is usually filled with enthusiasm for school. Teachers and parents will praise him for his beginning clumsy artwork, and the songs and poems he learns will find an enthusiastic and uncritical audience among his parents and grandparents. How could it be that any child would not respond positively?

When we see children in early elementary grades who appear to lack motivation, our ears should perk up to listen for the sounds of the zebra's hoofbeats. The *apparent* lack of motivation in most cases has nothing at all to do with motivation. After all, how do we decide that a child is not motivated? We see him fail to complete his assignments and not follow through on tasks. A child may also tell us he does not like school, but such complaints rarely occur until after the child has already experienced frustration and failure.

So in most cases, no one directly measures motivation itself. We assess it indirectly. We infer its presence or absence on the basis of what a child does. We observe the child's failure to complete schoolwork, and it looks to us as though he is not motivated. Failure to complete the work is, of course, the result of short attention span, distractibility, and other symptoms of ADD.

Once again we see how easy it is for a mistaken conclusion to lead parents and educators in the wrong direction. If a child's failure to finish schoolwork is regarded as a motivational problem, efforts will be directed toward motivating him. The goal will be wrong. Perhaps behavior modification or reward programs will be instituted. Punishment or withdrawal of privileges will be used as incentive. In the long run, these procedures will not do much good. In fact, treating a child with ADD this way will breed resentment, frustration, and further failure. Parents and teachers will also experience increased frustration and anger because their plans are unsuccessful. At times these feelings may lead to subtle, and sometimes not so subtle, rejection of the child. Punishment should play only a minor role in discipline of a child with ADD. Parents and teachers must be extra cautious to avoid punishing a child for something he cannot help, behavior that is a result of a physical handicap.

These patterns of punishment based on lack of understanding of the significance of the symptoms of Attention Deficit Disorder usually get started early in a child's life but become more of a problem when a child begins school as adults search, often frantically, for ways to force the child to complete schoolwork. Unfortunately, while all the inappropriate and harmful procedures are being used to try to change the child's behavior, the underlying problem, ADD, is being neglected.

When a teacher encounters any behavior that appears to reflect lack of motivation, he or she should not ask, "How can we motivate this child?" That question will lead nowhere. A different question should be asked—"What is it that interferes with the child's motivation?" That question will lead the teacher to consider a wide range of possibilities and, it is hoped, will lead to more constructive solutions.

Attention Deficit Disorder is not the only problem that interferes with a child's performance in school and causes him to appear unmotivated.

Learning disabilities, limited intelligence, anxiety, depression, family problems, and a host of other physical and psychological disorders also make a child appear unmotivated. Attention Deficit Disorder is one of the most common causes, however. Because ADD is chronic—that is, it persists year after year—it is usually relatively straightforward to distinguish apparent lack of motivation resulting from ADD from apparent lack of motivation resulting from other causes.

In older children it is more difficult to sort out lack of motivation from what interferes with motivation. By the time a child is in sixth or seventh grade, and especially by the time he reaches high school, motivation does play an important role in the quality of the child's schoolwork. Even here, however, the teacher should keep ADD in mind, because with older children it is still worth asking the question, "What interfered with motivation?" Often it was a failure to recognize ADD or other problems at an earlier age.

ADD and Level of Intelligence

There is no relationship between intelligence and ADD. Our experience suggests that there are an equal number of children with ADD among the mentally retarded and the intellectually gifted.

There are additional problems in recognizing ADD in children of especially low or high ability, but the principles of diagnosis and management remain the same. As young children get older they can sit still for longer periods of time, pay attention better, and control their own behavior. Since children of limited intelligence develop more slowly than those with normal intelligence, they may be more active or impulsive or have a shorter attention span than other children their age. Careful attention must be paid to differentiating between symptoms suggestive of ADD and those behaviors that are a result of the child's limited intelligence and slower development.

Very bright children may learn ways to compensate for some of the symptoms of ADD and may also offer creative, but incorrect, explanations to account for the difficulty they have completing their schoolwork. Parents, teachers, and doctors are often misled at first. In addition, there is a folk myth that says bright children, if bored, will behave in a way that is similar to that of a child with Attention Deficit Disorder. While it is certainly true that many bright children get bored with a regular school curriculum, boredom does not yield the pervasive, long-standing pattern of symptoms we see in ADD. In fact, if an enriched program does not help a child complete assignments and control his behavior better in the classroom, this should be regarded as an indication that the bright child might have Attention Deficit Disorder, and the diagnosis should be pursued with professional help.

Homework

Homework causes problems in many families. Even years after Attention Deficit Disorder is diagnosed, parents may still not fully understand or accept the impact of ADD on a child's ability to complete schoolwork. For the younger child, homework often consists of worksheets and other assignments that have not been completed in school. For middle and high school students, homework includes not only work undone, but regular assignments as well. These often include projects that must be completed over a period of several days or weeks. These longer projects are especially difficult because the extended period of time only adds to the lack of structure, which results in more unfinished assignments.

Homework, of course, is important in and of itself, but it takes on even greater significance in families with children with ADD because it is often the major source of conflict leading to serious family difficulties. We often encounter parents who tell us the worst problem they have to deal with is lying. When we trace the source of the child's lies we find most of them arose over conflict about schoolwork. Parents ask a child if he has homework, or they ask how things are going at school. A child lies and says he has no homework, and that school is going just fine. Later notes, progress reports, and report cards tell the sad, true story. Then arguments develop over honesty and trust.

There are other ways that homework causes trouble in family relationships. For example, parents may try to control a child's schoolwork, especially completion of homework, by withholding his allowance, restricting certain privileges, or, for the older child, denying access to the family car. Then heated arguments develop about these issues. All family members come to feel overwhelmed by a myriad of problems. Everyone loses sight of the fact that much of the anger and bitterness can be traced back to the original problem of getting schoolwork done.

There are several reasons why children with ADD fail to complete schoolwork. The first reason is a direct expression of the symptoms of ADD. Since the child finds it difficult to concentrate and organize himself, schoolwork does not get done. Second, children become angry and resentful over parents' efforts to control their behavior, especially if those efforts are punitive and consist of grounding or withdrawal of privileges. In these circumstances children readily develop negative attitudes toward schoolwork and dig in their heels, resisting more and more.

A third reason reflects the child's lack of confidence and fear of failure that develop after a while. If a child faces continual criticism, poor grades, and the feeling he is not smart enough or good enough to get the job done, he will give up. He may not want to try in the first place. Why even try if it never seems to go right? What adult would be willing to continue at a job that was filled with failure and criticism every day?

We have found that the main mistake parents and teachers make is to confuse these three causes of school-related problems. This leads to misdirected efforts to solve the problem. Usually it is fairly easy to recognize a bad attitude or resistance to schoolwork, but it is much more difficult to see at a glance how that bad attitude began in the first place. So once again, as in so many other things we have discussed in this book, parents and teachers may be tempted to view incomplete schoolwork as a discipline problem. For a child with Attention Deficit Disorder, that is a serious error.

There is only one way to help a child with ADD complete schoolwork. Note again the emphasis on the word "help." This is not a discussion of how to force your child to complete homework—that cannot be done. Parents often ask, "How can we get our child to understand how important it is to do schoolwork/homework?" Do you really think your child does not understand? Or has not learned the importance of education? Of course the child has learned and understands. Keep in mind your goals—we often ask the wrong questions. Here the question is, "How can we *help* the child get the work done?"

The steps to be followed are deceptively simple. Most parents will have already tried a similar technique. It is best if such a procedure can be instituted and maintained from the very early days of a child's school career, but it can be put into practice at any stage. Simply stated, parents and teachers must offer to the child their own ability to concentrate and organize things. They must substitute their greater frustration tolerance for the child's. This requires considerable cooperation between parent and teacher, and at times, unfortunately, this cooperation is difficult to obtain.

Teachers must send a note home each day that outlines what work the child must complete. This is quite a demand on a teacher's time and commitment, but there is no other way to do it. The child is the messenger, but the teacher must accept the responsibility for giving the child the message to be delivered.

Unfortunately, we often hear teachers say they do not want to use the daily-note procedure because a child in, say, fifth or sixth grade is too old for that sort of thing. Other teachers argue that if you do send notes on a daily basis, the child will never learn responsibility. Teachers who make such comments do not understand the nature of the Attention Deficit Disorder. It is not a matter of maturation, responsibility, or learning. The problem is based in a fundamental disability that is rooted in the way in which a child's central nervous system works. Although ADD, as we have said, is not a disease or an illness, it is a reflection of the physiology and biochemistry of the child's nervous system. We would no more expect a child with ADD to be "responsible," in the sense that he will accept all of the responsibility for completing his schoolwork, than we would expect a child who uses a wheelchair to accept the "responsibility" to walk on his own.

We have heard many teachers advise parents to withdraw their supervision or their help with homework because of the fear that the child will learn to rely upon it. It is true that children with ADD, because they require so much extra attention and supervision, can become dependent on their parents or others and either give up their independence or never develop well in this way in the first place. We must certainly remain vigilant to see to it that such a situation does not develop.

Nonetheless, we must remain equally cautious about allowing our concerns about the child's dependency to serve as an excuse for failing to provide him with all of the help, support, and guidance he really needs. It is natural for you, after sitting with your child while he does his homework, or for his teacher, after supervising him one-to-one for a long period of time, to start wondering when he will begin to learn to do his schoolwork by himself. We must, however, keep forever in mind the fact that the child's inability to follow through, to stay organized, and to get things done by himself does not reflect irresponsibility, immaturity, or the lack of a skill that he can learn. It is a handicap associated with ADD which may require compensatory help of teachers and parents throughout the child's school career.

As we develop a program for getting homework done, it is well to keep in mind that we are walking a thin line between pushing a child too hard to do things he simply cannot do because of his Attention Deficit Disorder and allowing him to get away with things that any child would be happy to take advantage of. This latter threat is what makes teachers and parents leery at times and makes them reluctant to offer an accommodation or adjustment of the child's curriculum. Adults fear the child is getting away with something. There is no clear-cut way to determine exactly how much homework a particular child is able to do or exactly how long the child may be able to sit, with or without supervision, and pore over a math textbook. You can only get close to the truth by, at times, requiring a little more than the child can do, and at times, probably making a mistake and letting him get away with a little less than he can do. Little by little, however, any parent can come to understand with reasonably accuracy how much a child can actually handle.

We recognize that the child's difficulty with homework or other aspects of schoolwork reflects not only the Attention Deficit Disorder but also all of the normal feelings and attitudes that all children bring to their school, as well as the discouragement and problems coping with failure that build up in the years before the child's ADD is recognized. One of the most important reasons for helping a child succeed with schoolwork is to show him that he is capable of doing the work and to create within him the feeling of satisfaction and pride that, in turn, automatically takes care of some attitude problems. Fear of failure, for example, is diminished when a child sees that he is not stupid, he can do the work, and he can get it done on time and in an acceptable manner. As fear of failure diminishes, much of the conflict over schoolwork also is reduced. We see less passive/aggressive behavior from children and less resistance in general to the things parents want them to do.

Let us return to a step-by-step outline of how to use the daily-note system. Each day, the teacher must send home a note listing incomplete assignments or other work that is to be completed before the next day. Depending on the child's age, a certain period of time, say, from ½ hour to 1½ hours, is set aside for a parent and child to work together on homework.

Children vary in how much supervision they need. Some will require little assistance, but others will need daily help throughout their school career. This is a major commitment for a parent, but there are no halfway measures. It is usually necessary for the child to do schoolwork with the parent present. Others will be able to do the work in their own room with only occasional supervision. Certain studies will require careful attention and cooperative effort between child and parent. In other cases, a parent's mere presence at the table will be sufficient to provide the structure the child needs. Parent and teacher have to work out a system of communication. It is best if each day a parent signs the homework note or writes some comments before the child brings it back to the teacher.

Cooperatively plan adjusted expectations for the child. It is best to see how much homework is realistic. Accept whatever work can be done during a specific amount of time. Many children with ADD find it so difficult to concentrate or are so disorganized that to complete the normal amount of schoolwork would be impossible. Adjustments have to be made in what is required.

Learning how much your child can do is not as difficult as it might seem at first. After you have worked at the kitchen table with your child for three or four weeks, you will have a very good idea of whether your child can work for 30 minutes or an hour. You will know when frustration begins to build. You will know when you are no longer accomplishing anything constructive and have reached a point that leads nowhere except to anger and tears. You can never be absolutely certain that your child is not feigning fatigue or manipulating you with his anger. As we noted above, some days you will probably press a little too hard, and some days you may allow your child to get away with something. We never know exactly where that dividing line is. But if you are careful and work at this consistently over a period of weeks and months, you will develop a good feel for where this dividing line is.

Throughout this book we have urged parents and teachers to adjust expectations and be flexible in managing children with Attention Deficit Disorder. We have stressed the importance of avoiding punishing a child for failure that results from a physical handicap. In the matter of homework, however, we urge you to develop very strict standards. We would never suggest that you punish a child for a failing grade that resulted from the symptoms of ADD. We do think, however, that it is reasonable to use firm discipline to force your child to work with you on homework every night. The child who fails a spelling test after diligent study should not be punished. The child who refuses to practice spelling words the night before the test should be forced to face the consequences of his resistive behavior. The consequences can be in the form of loss of some privilege or other punishment. So be strict about forcing your child to work with you, but be accommodating in your response to grades and quality of schoolwork if the poor quality reflects the ADD alone.

Many children will try to avoid homework. They will say that their teacher did not give them the note today, or they will insist there was no homework assigned. Develop a plan that is foolproof, so opportunities for manipulation do not get out of hand. This is one reason for having a note sent every day—there can be no manipulation. If parent or teacher is derelict in the responsibility because of being busy or forgetful on occasion and they do not send the note back and forth, most children will jump at the opportunity to use this adult lapse. On subsequent occasions they may report that the teacher forgot or thought no note was necessary or that mother did not sign the card this day.

We suggest that parents make an effort to have a second set of schoolbooks at home. These may be old editions obtained from the school or library. Sometimes it is possible to buy the books from a publisher. If actual textbooks and workbooks are not available, there are many items commercially available that are similar. We want to make sure the child cannot avoid schoolwork. This is not just an issue of punishment or discipline. It is also a matter of protecting the child against himself. A child who is tempted to lie his way out of circumstances and is prevented from doing so is also prevented from having one more negative experience.

It is usually sufficient to tell children they are expected to spend a certain amount of time on homework each evening. Although the teacher must be willing to supervise young children, older children can usually remember their books. As an added incentive, we have found it effective never to allow the child to use as an excuse the fact that he left his books at school. On those days that the child tries this excuse, we recommend you use the duplicate books and increase the amount of time the child is expected to spend on schoolwork for that one evening. Make the increase modest—add 10 or 15 minutes. The important message to give the child is that there is no way to avoid the responsibility and if he tries, he winds up in worse circumstances than he was in originally.

A program like this can be effective for children at any age. It is more complicated and difficult to implement in junior and senior high school because more teachers are involved. Often the child's counselor or special education teacher must accept the responsibility for coordinating this system. Older children resist more.

There are also times in a child's life when such a strict system will not be necessary. Be cautious. This is a difficult program to implement. Even though the idea is simple and straightforward, many of you have already tried it and found it difficult. The plan demands daily attention over a period of months and even years. As a consequence, it is easy to begin to wonder whether it is all worth it or to allow some of your vigilance to lapse because of the tedium or frequent conflict with your child.

Also, the system may work well for a while. As long as it is working, parents and teachers may relax and not be as diligent in maintaining every detail. This is often what accounts for failure. Attention Deficit Disorder is a chronic problem; it goes on and on. The steps necessary to help the child with ADD also must go on and on.

We want to highlight one other element inherent in this system. We believe such a note supervision system makes clear the distinction between the necessary accommodations to adjust expectations for the child with ADD and those requirements that are necessary to teach the child responsibility and self-reliance. Our goals with this system are to get as much work done as possible and to teach the child to make an effort and stick to it. Using the note system we can accomplish both of these goals, getting as much schoolwork done as possible while we teach the child that he must accept a certain degree of responsibility, within the limits of his capabilities. We can accomplish both goals without being punitive.

Home and School Cooperation

Children learn best when their education is a cooperative effort between home and school. Because children with learning disabilities and Attention Deficit Disorder encounter so much frustration and failure from year to year, parents often feel a great deal of disillusionment and dissatisfaction with the way their child is being managed in school. Teachers, too, become frustrated and discouraged. Beware of the trap of blaming the school for your child's difficulty. As we have noted above and in preceding pages, there are certainly errors in instruction and child management that may creep into your school's work with your child. Nonetheless, over the years, we have worked with teachers, education specialists, and administrators in countless schools in dozens of school districts. Of course, there are occasional teachers who are inefficient or ineffective. And there are occasionally brilliant, gifted, dedicated teachers to balance the teachers of questionable value. But for the most part, we have, time and again, been impressed with the sincerity, concern, and dedication of classroom teachers. It is rare to encounter teachers who do not care or who treat their responsibility to your children superficially or indifferently. Bear in mind that they, too, suffer the frustrations you have experienced that come from dealing with a problem of a chronic nature that goes on and on and must be met and dealt with each day with as much enthusiasm and commitment as on the very first day.

Given this frustration, parents and teachers often wind up blaming each other. Misunderstandings may arise because of failure to understand the chronic, long-term nature of the problem or failure to appreciate some of the subtle handicaps of the child with ADD and learning disabilities.

There are no simple rules or guidelines we can offer to eliminate this problem. It will remain a problem as long as children have learning disabilities. The goal of every parent and every teacher must be to keep in mind this delicate and sensitive issue and to realize how important it is that when problems arise between home and school, they be dealt with in a constructive, problem-solving way, rather than in a manner that emphasizes blame and assignment of responsibility for failure. Schools and parents work better as collaborators, not adversaries.

There are occasions when there are legitimate differences of opinion between parents and special education personnel. Special education laws in every state in the United States set out clearly the parents' rights. There are steps they can take to ask for a hearing or to appeal educational decisions with which they disagree. Nonetheless, legal steps are necessary in only a small fraction of cases and in most instances, parents and school personnel, in good will, can work together constructively to provide an optimum learning experience for the child with learning disabilities.

5 Preventing Problems at Home

The emotional swings of a child with ADD are hard on the whole family. Everyone has to be alert and make a continuing effort at prevention of problems rather than scolding or punishing after the event. This approach to a child with ADD is often the most difficult for parents, because it requires patience and wisdom that are easy to write about in a book like this, but which are very difficult to master in day-to-day, real-life situations. Nonetheless, mastering some of the ideas presented in this chapter will be among the most important aspects of living harmoniously with your youngster with ADD.

It is more difficult to develop a plan for appropriate discipline for a child with ADD for several reasons. First, no matter how sophisticated a parent (or teacher) might be, it is never possible to be certain to what extent troublesome behavior directly reflects ADD symptoms or habits that have been learned along the way. Consequently, the disciplinarian is always in the position of being less certain about how strict to be, how much to ignore, and what expectations to have than when dealing with other children.

A second problem for those who care for children with ADD is that it is often hard to be sure whether you are having any effect at all on a child with ADD. In most cases with an average child, even one who misbehaves from time to time, a few stern words, occasional punishment, and reasonable consistency will bring the behavior into line. A similar strategy will work to some extent with a child with ADD, but because of the child's poor impulse control and emotional lability, behavior problems are constantly renewed. The disciplinarian may wonder whether there is any impact on the child at all.

Many traditional notions of child rearing have to be set aside or modified. Consider the simple example of giving your child responsibility for taking the garbage out to the street once a week. If you have already tried this, you will recognize your family in the following description. No matter how many times you ask him to take a garbage can or a plastic bag to the street on a certain day or at a certain time, it never seems to get done. If you raise your voice or ask him to do it this minute and then supervise him, he will usually do it; any other technique does not seem to work. In fact, most parents say their child will trip and fall over the garbage 10 times and still walk past it without picking it up and carrying it to the street.

What is a parent to do? Keep in mind that most children do not set out to be defiant. Their inability to follow through on a simple task such as this does not reflect serious psychological problems or even a problem in their relationship with you, the parents. Rather, your youngster with ADD, like most other children, probably intends to do it right. When he sees the garbage, he means to take it out to the street, although his mind usually jumps to something else, and if he thinks about it at all, he probably tells himself he'll get back to it in a moment. Of course, that moment never comes, and the job never gets done.

You, as a parent, have to make a decision. First, consider what you want to accomplish. If your goal is to get the garbage out to the street, that's one thing. But, if your goal is to teach your child to do it responsibly, on his own, every week at a certain time, that is a different goal, and if that is your goal, you are probably in trouble. If you want the garbage taken out to the street, gently tell your child the next time the garbage is ready, "Son, the garbage here has to be taken out to the street, and we'd like you to do it right now, because if you don't, it might not get done." What such an approach means, of course, is that every week you are going to have to accept the responsibility of organizing this task for your child.

If, like many parents, you say at this point, "But when will he learn the responsibility himself?" you are focusing on the wrong aspect of the problem. Your child with ADD is probably not irresponsible, at least no more irresponsible than any other child. Certainly all children have to be taught to be responsible. Unfortunately, the symptoms associated with the Attention Deficit Disorder syndrome create behaviors and habits which often look like irresponsibility and bad attitude, but are not. These behavior problems require creative, careful, constructive planning by parents to see to it that the work gets done, the child gets a feeling of satisfaction about a job well done, and parents do not feel exploited or helpless.

Problems are best prevented, rather than dealt with after they occur. Guiding your child to the street with the garbage prevents the confrontation over why he did not do it. In most cases the key to prevention is to avoid the situation that produces the problems in the first place. It is also helpful to learn to avoid circumstances that produce excitement. If that is not possible, you have to prepare for things that cannot be avoided and recognize impending emotional upset. This may involve analyzing the times when your child is likely to get upset and think of ways to forestall this. If, for example, he gets into trouble just before dinner, maybe he should eat dinner earlier or have a bigger after-school snack. If there is trouble late in the evening, maybe he should go to bed earlier. You can see that suggestions of this type, when applied to your child, may require some major alterations in the routines of your family. You may not like doing it. You may even resent having to go to all that extra effort for a child who already has created more than his fair share of trouble for the family. The decision is yours. The important point we want to make is that this is an essential part of managing a youngster with ADD. The peace of mind and tranquility that comes for most families is worth the extra effort.

Your child's Attention Deficit Disorder is a physical handicap. It has to be recognized as such. Just because it is not as visible a handicap as, say, a limp or some other physical disability, makes it no less significant and certainly does not make your child any more to blame for his handicap. If your child limped because one leg was shorter than the other, and consequently he could not win races, you would not punish him, call him a bad boy, or tell him that he is an irresponsible athlete. Yet many parents, when faced with a youngster with ADD who cannot control his impulses or whose inability to organize and coordinate his own activities causes him continually to fail to take out the garbage or complete his homework, blame that child and regard his problem behavior as reflecting some deficiency in his attitude or character that can be remedied with harsh criticism. Try to avoid direct confrontation about trivial things. You can find a dividing line between letting your child get away with small things that trouble you and giving him so much freedom that he learns bad habits or does not learn proper ways of behaving.

Hyperactive youngsters seem to fall apart over unexpected changes in plan. Try to prevent disaster by anticipating ways that you can tone this down. This usually means more careful preparation for changes in routines. It involves careful explanation and even a second explanation about what is going to happen, even though another child may not require it. Recognize that unexpected changes of plans may cause more disruption in the life of your child with ADD, and direct your efforts toward settling him down rather than criticizing him for his overreaction. Always be on guard to avoid confrontations and trouble unless it is an issue that is absolutely essential. This is not easy advice to follow. It requires a strong commitment and a lot of practice. Also, some parents get upset when they hear this sort of advice because they think they might teach their children bad habits this way. If carefully done, that will not happen. It is often more important to keep things calm than it is to seize every little opportunity to demonstrate to the child that he is not living up to your expectations.

Nonpunitive Discipline

A challenge parents and educators face daily is to find discipline techniques and management strategies that are strict but do as little as possible to frustrate the child or injure his already fragile self-esteem. We must be ever vigilant, searching for ways to ally ourselves with the child against the problems he runs into, rather than allow ourselves to become identified, in the child's mind, as part of the problem.

The best way to begin is to look for ways to allow your child to face the natural consequences of behavior. Take, as an example, a 10-year-old boy who repeatedly fails to put his bicycle in the garage in the evening. His father becomes increasingly annoyed, fearing that he may drive over the bike because he cannot see it and worried the bike might be stolen. Everyone can come up with a similar personal example. How many times do you remind your child of the dangers to the bicycle? How many times do you think you have to explain before he will catch on?

Natural consequences teach best. Explain the problem to your child. Explain the risks he is taking. Then stop. We are tempted to explain too many things to our children too many times—especially if they seem to ignore us. The problem is rarely that you have not been heard or understood.

Now, imagine the bike is stolen; what do you do then? Keep in mind that even though the child himself may be to blame because of his negligence, he is going to be angry and upset. Far too often in our experience, parents make an unfortunate decision at this point. They see it as an opportunity to finally hammer home the lesson that the child's negligence caused the bike to be lost. The child knows it is his fault, of course. Even a 10-year-old of average intelligence can figure out that the bike was stolen as a natural consequence of his own behavior. We want him to understand that. However, if you view it as an opportunity to teach the same old lesson, your child has only two ways of dealing with his feelings.

He may feel so guilty and inadequate that our lecture serves to strip him of the last remnants of his self-esteem and makes him feel worse about himself than ever. But, remember, he has all that anger and hurt bottled up inside because his bicycle is gone. Then you jump in with your blame and recriminations and become a very tempting target for his anger. So, instead of examining his own behavior to see where he went wrong, he now has a convenient target to get angry with and blame.

Precisely the same pattern occurs time and time again in the life of the 15-year-old who brings home a report card with several failing grades. She may be angry, frustrated, bewildered, and, although she may not let you see it, hurt by those grades. If you choose that moment to be especially critical, you become a lightning rod for all of the misery she feels. You become an easy target and an easy excuse for the blame. So your teenager says to you, "The reason I get these bad grades is because you're on my back all the time. If you'd leave me alone, I would do better."

Let us take a closer look at two unnecessary and potentially harmful things that happen in these and similar circumstances. First, the child is denied an opportunity to take a critical look at his own behavior and learn from it. It is true, of course, that the child is his own worst enemy. He is the one who may refuse to examine his own behavior. Heaven knows, you have been trying long enough to get him to take an honest and objective look at the way he acts and how it gets him into trouble. Nonetheless, the child's failings should not blind you to the critical role you play when you respond to problems such as these in a harsh, critical, or rejecting manner.

The second unfortunate consequence in these situations is the lost opportunity for an adult to establish an alliance with the child against the problem. If this can be done, it keeps the adult-child relationship strong and positive and, at the same time, helps the child fight some of the frustration, bewilderment, and loss of self-esteem that inevitably occur.

Children often do a good job of hiding their feelings. We have heard parents say again and again, "What he does wouldn't be so bad if only it seemed like he cared." Although there may be a minority of children who truly do not care about their own behavior or its effect on others, the majority of children desperately care. It is because they feel so helpless about changing anything that they learn to hide their feelings and build a superficial shell around themselves that they hope will not only protect them from the outside world, but will also preserve dignity and self-respect.

What, then, is an alternative way to respond to a child with ADD?

We will offer several examples of different ways to deal with the children in our examples. We want to emphasize, however, that these are not gimmicks to be applied to isolated problems. Finding a way to establish an alliance with your child so that you can work together on problems must reflect a genuine commitment on your part. This must include recognition that ADD is a chronic problem that invades every corner of a child's life. The most practical help you can provide goes well beyond solving day-to-day problems and includes efforts that will make clear to your child that you understand the problem, that you do not blame the child for his handicap, and that you will work together, despite the continuing frustration you and the child experience with the child's symptoms.

Return to the stolen bicycle. The wise parent bites his tongue and resists the temptation to remind the child that he would not be in these straits if he had followed parental advice. Instead, go to your child, put your arm around his shoulder, and let him know you understand how bad he feels about the loss of his bicycle. Let him know that you share his frustration and feelings of loss. Let him know that you sympathize with how bad he feels. Tell him, "I know how important your bike was to you. If you want me to, I'll help you save up money to buy another. I have several ideas about how you can earn some money, and there are extra chores around the house your mother and I will pay you for."

You have to be sincere. These are not clever words to be used to manipulate your son. He will still be upset. He will not greet what you say with joy. But if you approach the problem this way, you establish a partnership with your child. If he is still tempted to blame you or refuses to accept responsibility for his own behavior, let it pass without comment. Follow through with support and positive emphasis to prevent the more serious consequence of having your child identify you as part of the problem.

If you follow this advice, do not expect your son to suddenly turn over a new leaf and always remember to put his possessions in the garage or lock them safely away. After all, this is not a memory problem in the first place. Nor will he "learn" his lesson. This is not a learning problem. He will simply be better able to profit from the experience because you have kept your conflict out of the problem arena. You have not muddied the water with other issues. If you can follow through with many other less dramatic and often less clear-cut examples in the same way, eventually a pattern will be established that will allow for your child's growth and self-understanding, as well as strengthen your relationship with him.

Such a "non-intervention" strategy has to be applied with good judgment. While it may be appropriate to allow a 10-year-old child to suffer the natural consequences of a stolen bicycle, we cannot let the same child face, on his own, the consequences of his failure to complete schoolwork. We have already addressed the issue of helping with homework. By the time a child is, say, 15 years old, however, there is little that parents or teachers can do to force him to do his schoolwork. Each case has to be decided based on your knowledge of your child, but you reach a point in which the same judicious steps must be taken to allow a teenager to face the natural consequences of his own behavior in school. That may mean failing a course, being suspended from school, or even being dismissed from school for a semester, as unfortunate and regrettable as that may be. It is often preferable to getting involved in destructive fights and arguments at home. If you choose to fight, you may inflame things further. Then, if a child fails or drops out of school, relationships with teachers and parents have become so strained the child finds it difficult to recover, to get his own life on track again, and to resume his education. Keep your eye on your goals. Today's grade on an exam or in a course may be much less important than a child's opinion about himself or his overall attitude toward education.

We were impressed with the behavior of the assistant principal in one of the high schools in our community. He was responsible for attendance and discipline. His management of all students, those with problems and those without, was characterized by firmness, fairness, and consistency. For example, the school had a rule that a student was allowed five unexcused absences per term. If a child exceeded that number, he was dropped from the class for that semester. There were no exceptions. Equally important, there was no additional punishment in the form of either school restrictions or criticism. Parents were counseled and encouraged to be supportive and urge their children to attend class and complete their assignments, but not to add additional punishment if a student was dismissed from class.

This man's approach to his students was honest and straightforward. He could look a student in the eye or put his hand on a boy's shoulder and say, "You're having a problem getting to class. You've exceeded the five unexcused absences and are being dropped from that class. I'm here to help you. If you want to work out something with me to make sure you can get to the rest of your classes this semester, or if next term you need my help keeping to a schedule, let me know." He was always available. If he saw a student in the hall, even if he had disciplined him a few days before, he would talk to him, be supportive, and indicate his availability to help without being overbearing.

Many students credited this man's method of dealing with attendance and other discipline problems with being the reason that, although they were angry and frustrated with school at the time, they did not develop an overall negative attitude toward school that would affect them later on in life. A number of the students from that school have been our patients, and they have told us how this sort of experience made them willing to take another chance on school at a later date or made them feel that it was worth trying a course again the next semester.

Some parents and teachers may be alarmed at our suggestion that they not put up a stronger fight to keep a child in class or in school. That would be a misinterpretation of what we are suggesting. Our point is that it is not all that difficult to recognize the point when, after fighting, arguing, threatening, disciplining, grounding, crying, and grinding your teeth, you know you are no longer being effective in getting your child to do what you want. At that point, recognize there may be more to be gained by allowing the child to face the natural consequences of his behavior and establishing that alliance with him against the problem than there is by continuing with useless and potentially destructive confrontations.

Schedules

Scheduling your child's activities is often helpful. Like so many other bits of advice we have offered, this one, too, requires a great deal of your time and effort. Scheduling your child's activities during free time has to take into consideration his impulsivity and his inability to organize things himself. Young children with ADD often benefit from a schedule such as the following:

3:00—Arrive home from school, have milk and cookies
3:15—Do homework
3:30—Go outside to play ball
4:00—Do homework
4:15—Practice piano
4:30—Go outside to play
5:30—Read
And so forth.

This sort of schedule does not work as well with older children because you cannot control their schedules as well. Notice that there are longer time periods and more total time for play than for homework and practicing the piano. This takes into consideration the child's limited attention span and lower threshold of frustration. Of course, you are going to have to enforce that schedule. It is a way of getting things done so that by suppertime homework is not still hanging over the child's head and parents are not facing the evening with dread, wondering what kind of fight is going to be caused by their insistence that the child do 15 minutes' worth of homework or practice the piano.

Schedules such as this have to be fairly strict but at the same time incorporate a great deal of flexibility. Some days there will be no homework. Some days there will be other activities to integrate into the schedule. If a child can read, he should have the schedule written out so he can consult it. Post it on the door of the refrigerator, the bulletin board, or a wall in his room. Post several copies. The advantage of seeing the schedule in written form is that it helps focus the child's attention. If it is written out, he can look at his schedule to see what has to be done. This helps organize his activities and makes it clearer and less confusing for him than if he had to carry the schedule around in his head.

This principle of writing things down for children with ADD can be applied in other areas as well. The more concrete and explicit, and the more that the notes or schedules add to the child's ability to organize his activities and understand what is expected of him at different times of the day, the better he will be able to meet those expectations and satisfy not only you, his parents, but himself as well. We must not lose sight of the idea that activities should be organized in order to arrange maximum success for the child. The value of getting homework completed and getting good grades is not just the value that comes from having the work done, but the satisfaction in the accomplishment this creates for the child with ADD. Life is full of failure and frustration for your son or daughter. Every time you create a success experience for him or her, you go a long way toward counteracting the negative effects of all the bad things that happen so often to your child.

Chip on the Shoulder Attitude

Parents often describe their child as if he always has a chip on his shoulder. By that, people mean he seems to be looking for a fight. As one mother expressed it, "It doesn't seem to matter what you say to him when he's in one of those moods, it's always the wrong thing to say." This chip on the shoulder attitude really comes from a self-esteem problem. Children with ADD usually lack confidence because they have had plenty of experience proving to them that they do not do things very well. This robs them of self-confidence, lowers their self-esteem, and makes them overly sensitive. Because of this oversensitivity, they readily interpret, or even misinterpret, as criticism even the most gentle things you may say. For example, your son may be watching television by himself, selecting the programs he wants without any concern for anyone else. After three hours, his sister comes into the room and asks if she can turn to a channel she would like to see. An argument starts and you try to intervene. It would be quite reasonable for you to say to your son, "Your sister should have a turn; you've been watching TV and having your own way for the past three hours." Why in the world should something as reasonable as that cause him to explode? The answer does not lie in what you have said, rather it lies in understanding your son. He has a long memory filled with many examples of times he has been criticized and treated in ways he thinks are unfair. If your family is typical, he always thinks his sister gets more privileges than he does and that she gets away with a lot of things you will not allow him to do. He is so sensitive to this issue that any time you criticize him in favor of his sister, even when it is fair and reasonable, he is not hearing about the one time such as the television example, but he immediately feels salt rubbed in the old wound of his sister being treated better than he is; that is why you see the reaction from him. It may seem unreasonable to you, but that is not going to change the way things are.

So how do you respond? What do you do? Some of his outbursts are going to have to be ignored. If you are satisfied that what you are doing is fair and reasonable, go ahead and enforce the rule. If your son makes a fuss, send him out of the room. He may take care of that for you by stomping out in a rage. Do not try to explain the logic of the situation to him then. He is not listening. And his feelings are not governed by the same logic you use. In many ways it could be said he sees the situation so differently than you do that it is not even possible to have a common-sense discussion with him at that moment. Later on, after he has settled down, try to explain it to him. Explain not only the fairness of what happened, but explain to him your understanding of how he feels unfairly treated compared to his sister, and that you know that that was part of his reaction over the TV that day.

Doing as we have suggested will not eliminate the problem. It will happen again and again and it will occur in different, but similar, circumstances. The positive effect will be to let your child know that you understand him, even if he is not able to express all of these feelings and ideas to you directly himself. It will keep this one episode about the television from adding to that large collection of injustices that your child has already collected and uses as proof about how badly he is treated. If you can keep him from adding further to this collection, you will make him feel a little bit more valued, a little less rejected, and a little more part of the family. This, then, becomes one small increment added to many, many other small increments that you will put together in order to make modest, but significant, changes in your child's behavior. Eventually, there will be a reduction in the frequency and intensity of the outbursts in similar situations.

Most parents find advice of this kind useful and are able to follow through on it. A problem arises when there are no immediate dramatic changes in a child's behavior. It is easy to slip back again into bad habits and feelings of discouragement that cause you eventually to give up on efforts that do not seem to have a payoff. After all, our discussion about how behavior is learned and the value of reinforcers applies to you as well. If you do not get a reward or a reinforcement for something you're doing, such as working constructively to try to change your child's behavior, why should you keep at it? So you have to work in the early stages at being your own reinforcer. Mother and father have to work together to reinforce each other. Early on, when you begin to try some of the ideas discussed in this book, you will get no reward other than to be able to say to yourself, "Well, I guess I feel a little less upset because I know I'm doing the right thing." Another reward that is worth a great deal comes when your spouse pats you on the shoulder, gives you a hug, and says, "I think you handled that very well." That ought to hold you for a while, and eventually you will begin to see some lessening in the tension in your house and some improvements in your child's relationship with brothers and sisters and with other children as well. Patience and persistence, Mother. Patience and persistence, Father. Take your reinforcers where you can find them. It can be a long and difficult road raising a child with ADD. But it is possible to do it in a constructive, mentally healthy way that will provide rich rewards for you and your child.

Parents with ADD and Their Children with ADD

We mentioned in Chapter 1 that Attention Deficit Disorder tends to run in families. That means there is an increased likelihood that one or both parents of a child with ADD will also have the disorder. No one has documented the precise extent of this heritability factor, but there is sufficiently high possibility that one of the parents of a child with ADD will also have the disorder that it should always be considered.

The dilemma faced by families with more than one member with ADD is often substantial. In such a case we are asking a parent who may be impulsive and short-tempered or emotionally labile, to be extra patient and understanding of a child with similar symptoms. The problem is made even more difficult by the fact that it is rare that the parent has ever been diagnosed. Not only does, say, the father not understand the significance of his own behavior, but the very symptoms of the ADD may create extra stress for that parent at work and may contribute to tension within the marriage.

Some adults with ADD have developed elaborate techniques to compensate for their problem. Without fully understanding the nature of the disorder, many adults learn to be overly organized or especially well-controlled. They do this because they realize they cannot allow themselves any room for error. Although they may not be able to define their problem as Attention Deficit Disorder, they know that they are forgetful if they don't keep lists of things, likely to become disorganized if they don't keep everything carefully in its place, and easily upset when things go wrong.

Consider the problem faced by the family with a husband and father who has learned to organize himself in such a way as a compensation for his ADD, of which he is not even aware, and a child with the very symptoms that threaten the structure and organization the parent struggles so desperately to protect. Expert consultation and diagnosis are essential in such cases. Just understanding why people behave the way they do, and where certain seemingly unexplainable behavior comes from, lessens tension and helps people find methods of coping.

Of course, compulsive organization is only one method of coping with ADD. There are many others. Some are helpful and some less so. Some methods can be harmful. It is important that both parents of a child with ADD examine their own behavior to see if they possibly have Attention Deficit Disorder. If so, it may be a good idea to get professional consultation for themselves.

The Need for Psychotherapy

How do you decide whether psychotherapy will be helpful for your child with ADD or your family? Most children with Attention Deficit Disorder do not require extensive psychological treatment. Nonetheless, many families find it immensely helpful to have several consultation sessions with a knowledgeable child psychologist in order to gain a better understanding of the disorder. This helps the child and other members of the family in their efforts to determine how the symptoms of ADD cause behavioral and learning difficulties.

It is our practice to meet several times with the child with ADD and other family members after the diagnosis has been made. This gives us an opportunity to discuss practical day-to-day matters of concern and explain how behavior patterns and relationships within the family are related to, and affected by, the Attention Deficit Disorder. We find that limited counseling of this sort is sufficient for many families. With their increased knowledge and understanding, they are able to work together better for everyone's benefit.

A substantial number of people require more extensive psychotherapy. Psychological treatment is not directed toward the Attention Deficit Disorder itself. That is a physical problem and is not changed by counseling or other psychological techniques. When more extensive psychological treatment is required, it is often because the relationships within the family have become so damaged that the family is unable to heal itself, even with the added understanding of the nature of ADD.

The child may require individual psychological treatment because of emotional problems that have developed as a result of having Attention Deficit Disorder. Self-esteem problems are common. In some children they are so severe as to cause depression or such discouragement with school and social relationships that the child withdraws or finds other self-destructive ways of dealing with his anguish. Attention Deficit Disorder can also cause crippling anxiety. Many children with ADD need help overcoming their frustration and anger.

Whether a child or family needs extensive psychotherapy or only short-term counseling, we remain available to the family as the years go on. It is a normal feature of Attention Deficit Disorder to encounter difficulties from time to time that the child or the family cannot solve themselves. This does not indicate that earlier psychotherapy was not effective, nor should it be taken as a sign that the child's disorder is getting worse. Rather, as children grow and enter different developmental stages and as families, as a whole, change and mature, the nature of family relationships and the demands made on individuals change. This may lead to a temporary increase in psychological symptoms in the child with ADD or troubles in family relationships. Once again, although in some instances more extensive psychological treatment is required, usually these problems can be managed with several counseling sessions with a child or family psychologist. The goal is to get the child and family back on the right track again.

Choose a child psychologist carefully. Not all psychologists or psychiatrists are interested in or experienced with Attention Deficit Disorder. Your physician will usually know of other professionals in the community who can provide high-quality care. If you are still uncertain, do not hesitate to make inquiries of your own. Call and ask to speak to the psychologist. Explain that you have a child with ADD. Describe the problems you are having. Ask straightforwardly whether the psychologist is experienced in these matters and thinks he or she can help you with the problem. Psychologists are not offended by such questions. On the contrary, they welcome them because it enables them to offer their services in those areas where they know they can be most effective.

6   *Future Adjustment of Children with ADD*

Many professionals who work with children with ADD and their families have tended to be rather pessimistic about the future of children with Attention Deficit Disorder. This pessimism, in part, reflected a lack of information as well as frustration over not being as helpful as most of us want to be. Many parents view the impulsive, seemingly irresponsible behavior of their children with ADD and become frightened as they contemplate the teenage years and adulthood. They often wonder, if we have this much trouble with him as a child, what is he going to be like when he's a teenager? As an adult, how is he ever going to be able to get a job and keep it?

We know that as adolescents, about 25 percent of all youngsters with Attention Deficit Disorder with Hyperactivity have problems with antisocial behavior such as fighting, occasional moderate marijuana use, and minor delinquency. Many also have failed a grade by this time, and overall their achievement is low compared to their classmates. What does the future hold for a child with Attention Deficit Disorder?

A child with ADD is at risk for later behavioral and psychological problems. There is no doubt about that, and we would do our children harmful disservice if we failed to acknowledge it. However, there are also some reassuring answers now available for our questions about the future, both from the clinical experience of professionals who work with children with ADD and their families, and from the results of several follow-up studies that have been reported recently in medical and psychological journals. Many children with ADD grow up to lead perfectly normal lives. One comprehensive study begun over 20 years ago at Children's Hospital in Montreal, Canada, provides some important information. There, pediatricians, psychologists, and psychiatrists studied what happened to a group of 75 children who had been diagnosed as hyperactive. (Remember there was no such diagnosis as ADD when the study began.) They kept in touch with the children and their families and brought them back to the hospital at regular intervals for interviews and medical and psychological testing.

The most recent report of the follow-up study was published in 1986 as a book, *Hyperactive Children Grown Up*, written by Gabrielle Weiss and Lily Trokenberg Hechtman. The study addressed two major questions. First, how do specific symptoms of the hyperactivity syndrome (ADD) affect life at work? Second, because it was well known that adolescent hyperactive children have a relatively low self-concept, how do they fare in terms of general psychological adjustment as young adults?

There were several hundred children in the original study, and 75 were followed for 20 years into young adulthood. During all that time, 10 of the 75 children had had 25 or more psychotherapy sessions. The remainder had between 10 and 25 interviews with professionals for a number of reasons. For most of them it was just routine discussions with pediatricians about health and medicine. For some, these interviews included crisis management, help with particular problems as they came up, and general follow-up as they were monitored over the 20-year period. So, 65 of the 75 had no elaborate psychotherapy or psychological counseling, but they had some advice along the way. Because the study was begun almost 20 years ago, none of the children received Ritalin. Twenty-seven of them were given the drug Thorazine. Six received Dexadrine, 9 a mixture of drugs, and 32 no drugs at all.

The results of the study were based on personality tests and self-rating questionnaires given to the children as young adults. Questionnaires also were given to high school teachers and employers. The results of these questionnaires and rating scales were then compared with the results of tests given to 75 other non-hyperactive young adults who served as a comparison group. Because these hyperactive children were followed over a number of years, it was possible to ask high school teachers the same questions that were ultimately asked of supervisors, foremen, and other people who were in a position to rate the work behavior of these young adults. For instance, a teacher might be asked, "Did he get his work done?" A supervisor on the job could be asked the same question. Teachers were asked, "Would you like this person in your classroom again?" "How did he get along with his classmates?" Similarly, employers were asked, "Are you pleased you hired this person? Would you do it again?" "Does he get along with his fellow workers?" So, not only was it possible to compare hyperactive young adults to non-hyperactive young adults, but it was possible to compare how these people did in the workplace with how they had done in school according to their teachers' reports.

The results of the study were encouraging. There was no difference on the employer questionnaires between children who had been diagnosed as hyperactive and those who served as the comparison group. It is interesting to see that many of the young men and women who were rated satisfactorily by employers had been badly rated by high school teachers. There was a difference in the ratings of teachers between the hyperactive children and the comparison group. But by the time they got out into the workplace, there was no difference. We will come back in a moment to some possible reasons for this and the practical implications for ways to achieve this for other children. Looking at the mental health of the young adults who had been classified as hyperactive when they were children, the researchers found no major significant psychological disturbances in the hyperactive group, but they tended to still be more pessimistic than the comparison group and more lacking in self-confidence. As a group, they also tended to have impaired social skills.

Overall, the results of this study of a large number of children over many years present some encouraging information for those of us concerned about children with ADD and hyperactivity and their families. Perhaps one of the most important findings is that the demands of school that the child with ADD often finds so terribly difficult to deal with may be different from the requirements of the workplace. Even though teacher and employer expect you to show up on time, work diligently until the job is completed, and be cooperative with co-workers, this does not seem to cause as much difficulty for the young adult on the job, even though similar demands in the last few years of high school seem to be something they could not handle very well.

About ⅓ to ½ of children with ADD continue to be plagued by the symptoms of the syndrome in adulthood. Adult problems, such as anti-social behavior and drug use, as might be expected, are more common in those individuals who continue, as adults, to have difficulty with short attention span, impulse control, and emotional lability.

We have reviewed the procedures and results of this study in some detail, because it is the most thorough long-term project that exists. In addition we wanted to highlight some of the encouraging features this research reports. They should be considered seriously by all who work with children with Attention Deficit Disorder. However, we must stress that significant problems exist for people with ADD and many, even those who receive excellent professional care in their early years, will continue to need some supportive psychological help as adults. Researchers Weiss and Hechtman describe Attention Deficit Disorder as a chronic, pervasive condition that appears to last throughout life. Among their more troubling findings is the fact that a significant percentage of their subjects, something in the neighborhood of 25 percent, have a history of some form of antisocial behavior. Some researchers have reported that adolescents with ADD consume more alcohol and abuse street drugs more frequently and to a greater extent than do their non-ADD peers. However, the research reported by the Montreal group found no evidence of alcoholism or significant drug addiction in adulthood as an outcome of the childhood syndrome.

Hyperactive Children Grown Up includes several chapters containing memories, impressions, and comments of the patients themselves.

Their views of what helped them are instructive. When adults were asked what had helped them most through their lives they chose most often an individual person (a parent, teacher, friend, or counselor) who had believed strongly in them. The majority had not liked taking medicine, mainly because they did not like being different or being embarrassed when other children found out. They felt they had not been given enough information about what the medicine was for and why they were taking it.

Can some guidelines be drawn from what we have learned? We know the disorder is wide-ranging and touches all aspects of the lives of those who have it. We know it does not go away. We know it makes growing up difficult and it makes living in the family with a child with ADD hard at times.

On the other hand, we know that some children with ADD are able to manage their first jobs well, despite the problems they had in school. Also, even though many people have problems as adults, no matter what study we read, we find the majority of adults with Attention Deficit Disorder lead normal lives.

So, if it is the case that some children with ADD can manage their first job well despite the problems associated with the ADD syndrome, what guidelines does this give us about how we ought to deal with the behavior problems we see earlier in their lives?

We think three points emerge quite clearly:

1. Families must get through the difficult times without being torn completely apart. Protect your family. Guard against hate and complete rejection. A time may even come for your family when it is best for your child to live elsewhere for a while. Even if that happens, it can be done constructively and with a minimum of bad feelings. Above all, protect the basic relationships in your family. In a few years they will provide the foundation for positive experiences for all of you again.

2. Protect your child from causing such serious damage to himself or his future that he cannot ever get his life back on track. We have in mind serious crime or drug use. Children can recover from many things, even from dropping out of school.

3. Provide as much as possible for keeping self-esteem as high as possible.

One of the most important ways to do this is to be ever mindful of ways to implement nonpunitive discipline. Every time you find a way to establish an alliance with your child, you strengthen a bond you enjoy and add to the child's sense of worth because he knows you care enough to be an ally. Be strict without being punitive or rejecting in a way that assaults a child's dignity.

There should be a fourth point, but it is so important that it runs through all three of those already listed. That is, families must learn to maintain a balanced point of view. Essential issues must be sorted from both the inconsequential and those which are important but can, without danger, be set aside. It is clearly not necessary to force every skipped class, failure to take the garbage out to the curb, messy room, or fight with a younger brother to a major confrontation and a test of wills that ultimately leads to great rancor. Such a course of action can lead to irreparable alienation among family members and a destructive assault to the self-esteem of the child with Attention Deficit Disorder.

In its simplest sense the advice is very easy to give to parents of children with ADD, but extraordinarily complex and often difficult to put into practice. Be as calm as possible, do not overreact, keep your eye on the future, and probably most important, get every last ounce of energy possible out of your sense of humor. Your child will probably survive and go on to live a reasonably normal life. Make sure that you, as parents, have the same future prospects: a life that will include a mutually rewarding, loving relationship with your adult child.

Sources for Additional Reading

Aarskog, D.; Fevang, F. O.; Klove, H.; et al. The effect of the stimulant drugs, dextroamphetamine and methylphenidate, on secretion of growth hormone in hyperactive children. *J Pediatrics* 90:136, 1977.

Ackerman, P. T.; Dykman, R. A.; and Peters, J. E. Teenage status of hyperactive and non-hyperactive learning disabled boys. *Amer J Orthopsychiatry* 47:577-596, 1977.

Adkins, L., and Cady, J. *Help! This Kid's Driving Me Crazy! (The Young Child with Attention Deficit Disorder)*. Danville, Illinois: The Interstate, 1986.

Alberts-Corush, J., et al. Attention and impulsivity characteristics of the biological and adoptive parents of hyperactive and normal control children. *Amer J Orthopsychiatry* 56:413-423, 1986.

Atkins, M. S., et al. A comparison of objective classroom measures and teacher ratings of Attention Deficit Disorder. *J Abnorm Child Psychol* 13:155-166, 1985.

Ballinger, C., et al. Effect of methylphenidate on reading in children with Attention Deficit Disorder. *Amer J of Psychiatry* 141:1590-1593, 1984.

Barkley, R. *Hyperactive Children—A Handbook for Diagnosis and Treatment*. New York: The Guilford Press, 1981.

Bloomingdale, L. (ed.). *Attention Deficit Disorder*. Jamaica, New York: SP Medical and Scientific Books, 1984.

Brown, R., et al. Methylphenidate and cognitive therapy: A comparison of treatment approaches of hyperactive boys. *J Abnorm Child Psychol* 13:66-73, 1985.

Brown, R. T., and Alford, N. Ameliorating attentional deficits and concomitant academic deficiencies in learning disabled children through cognitive training. *J Learn Disabil* 17(1):20-26, 1984.

Brown, R. T., and Sleator, E. K. Methylphenidate in hyperkinetic children: Differences in dose effects on impulsive behavior. *Pediatrics* 64:408-411, 1979.

Campbell, S., et al. Correlates and predictives of hyperactivity and aggression: A longitudinal study of parent-referred problem preschoolers. *J Abnorm Child Psychol* 14:217-227, 1986.

Campbell, S. B.; Endman, M. W.; and Bernfield, G. A three year follow up of hyperactive preschoolers into elementary school. *J Child Psychology and Psychiatry* 18:239-249, 1977.

Charles, L.; Schian, R.; and Zelniker, T. Optimal dosages of methylphenidate for improving the learning and behavior of hyperactive children. *J Develop and Behav Pediatrics* 2:78-81, 1981.

Conners, C. K. *Food Additives for Hyperactive Children.* New York: Plenum Press, 1980.

Conners, C. K., and Taylor, E. Pemoline, methylphenidate and placebo in children with minimal brain dysfunction. *Arch Gen Psychiatry* 37:922-930, 1980.

Denson, R.; Nanson, J.; and McWatters, M. Hyperkinesis and maternal smoking. *Canadian Psychiatric Association Journal* 20:183-187, 1975. *Diagnostic and Statistical Manual of Mental Disorders—DSM III*, ed. 3. American Psychiatric Association, Washington, D.C.

Firestone, P., et al. Vicissitudes of follow up studies: Differential effects of parent training and stimulant medication with hyperactives. *Amer J Orthopsychiatry* 56:184-194, 1986.

Firestone, P.; Kelly, M.; Goodman, J.; and Davey, J. Differential effects of parent training and medication with hyperactives. *J Child Psychiatry* 20:135-147, 1981.

Furukawa, C. P., et al. Learning and behavior problems associated with theophyllin therapy. *Lancet* 1:621, 1984.

Harsough, C., and Lambert, N. Medical factors in hyperactive and normal children: Prenatal, developmental and health history findings. *Amer J Orthopsychiatry* 52:190-201, 1985.

Holborow, P., and Berry, P. A multinational, cross-cultural perspective on hyperactivity. *Amer J Orthopsychiatry* 56(2):320-322, 1986.

Howell, D. Fifteen year follow up of behavioral history of Attention Deficit Disorder. *Pediatrics* 76:185-189, 1985.

Huessy, H. R., and Cohen, A. H. Hyperkinetic behaviors and learning disabilities followed over seven years. *Pediatrics* 57:4-10, 1976.

Johnston, M., and Singer, H. Brain neurotransmitters and neuromodulators in pediatrics. *Pediatrics* 70:57-69, 1982.

Kupietz, S.; Winsberg, B.; and Sverd, J. Learning ability and methylphenidate (Ritalin) plasma concentration in hyperkinetic children. *J Child Psychiatry* 21:27-30, 1982.

Margolis, H.; Brannigan, G. G.; and Poston, M. A. Modification of impulsivity: Implications for teaching. *Elementary School Journal* 77:231-237, 1977.

Mattes, J.; Boswell, L.; and Oliver, H. Methylphenidate effects on symptoms of Attention Deficit Disorder in adults. *Arch Gen Psychiatry* 41:1059-1067, 1984.

Milich, R., and Pelham, W. Effects of sugar ingested on the classroom and playgroup behavior of Attention Deficit Disordered boys. *J Consult Clin Psychology* 54:714-718, 1986.

O'Leary, S. G., and Pelham, W. E. Behavioral therapy and withdrawal of stimulant medication in hyperactive children. *Pediatrics* 61:211-217, 1978.

Palfrey, Judith, et al. The emergence of attention deficit in early childhood: A prospective study. *J Develop and Behav Pediatrics* 6:339-348, 1985.

Rachelefsky, G., et al. Behavior abnormalities and poor school performance due to oral theophyllin use. *Pediatrics* 78:1133-1138, December, 1986.

Rapoport, J. Dextro-amphetamine: Cognitive and behavioral effects in normal prepubertal boys. *Science* 199:560-562, 1978.

Rapport, Mark, et al. Attention Deficit Disorder with Hyperactivity: Differential effects of methylphenidate on impulsivity. *Pediatrics* 76:938-943, 1985.

Rapport, Mark; Stoner, G.; DuPaul, G.; et al. Methylphenidate in hyperactive children: Differential effects of dose on academic, learning and social behavior. *J Abnorm Child Psychol* 13:227-244, 1985.

Rie, H., and Rie, E. (eds.). *Handbook of Minimal Brain Dysfunctions: A Critical View.* New York: Wiley-Interscience, 1980.

Ross, D. M., and Ross, S. A. *Hyperactivity: Current Issues, Research & Theory.* 2d ed. New York: Wiley-Interscience, 1982.

Rourke, B. Issues in the neuropsychological assessment of children with learning disabilities. *Canadian Psychological Review* 17:89-102, 1976.

Safer, D., and Krager, M. Trends in medication treatment of hyperactive school children. *Clin Pediatrics* 22:500-504, 1983.

Satterfield, J. H.; Satterfield, B. T.; and Kentwell, D. Three-year multimodality treatment study of 100 hyperactive boys. *Pediatrics* 73:650-655, 1981.

Schain, C. L. A four year follow up study of the effects of methylphenidate on the behavior and academic achievement of hyperactive children. *J Abnorm Child Psychol* 9:495-505, 1981.

Schayitz, S., et al. Psychopharmacology of Attention Deficit Disorders: Pharmacokinetic, neuroendocrine, and behavioral measures following acute and chronic treatment with methylphenidate. *Pediatrics* 69:688-694, 1982.

Silver, A.; Hagin, R.; and Beecher, R. Scanning, diagnosis, and intervention in the prevention of reading disabilities. *J Learn Disabil* 11:437-449, 1978.

Silver, L. Acceptable and controversial approaches to treating the child with learning disabilities. *Pediatrics* 55:406-415, 1975.

Silver, L. *The Misunderstood Child: A Guide for Parents of Learning-Disabled Children.* New York: McGraw-Hill, 1984.

Sprague, R. L., and Sleator, E. K. Methylphenidate in hyperkinetic children: Differences in dose effects on learning and social behavior. *Science* 198:1274-1276, 1977.

Sprague, R. L., and Sleator, E. K. What is the proper dose of stimulant drugs in children? *Int J Ment Health* 4:75-105, 1975.

Stewart, M. A.; Mendelson, W. B.; and Johnson, N. E. Hyperactive children as adolescents: How they describe themselves. *Child Psychiatry and Human Development* 4:3-11, 1973.

Swanson, J. M., and Kinsbourne, M. Food dyes impair performance of hyperactive children on a laboratory learning test. *Science* 207:1485, 1980.

Swanson, J. M.; Kinsbourne, M.; and Roberts, W. Time-response analysis of the effect of stimulant medication on the learning ability of children referred for hyperactivity. *Pediatrics* 61:21-29, 1978.

Tryphonas, H., and Trites, R. Food allergy in children with hyperactivity, learning disabilities, and/or minimal brain dysfunction. *Annals of Allergy* 42:22-27, 1979.

Weiss, B.; Williams, J. H.; Margen, S.; et al. Behavioral responses to artificial food colors. *Science* 207:1487, 1980.

Weiss, G., and Hechtman, L. *Hyperactive Children Grown Up.* New York: The Guilford Press, 1986.

Wender, Esther. The food additive–free diet in the treatment of behavior disorders: A review. *J Develop and Behav Pediatrics* 7:35-42, 1986.

Werry, J. S.; Sprague, R. L.; and Cohen, M. N. Conners' Teacher Rating Scale for use in drug studies with children—An empirical study. *J Abnorm Child Psychol* 3:217-229, 1975.

Woolfolk, A. E., and Woolfolk, R. L. A contingency management technique for increasing student attention in a small group setting. *Journal of School Psychology* 12:204-212, 1974.

Glossary

Most technical words and other terms with which the reader may not be familiar are defined in the text. Included here are shorter definitions for quick reference, as well as a number of other terms frequently encountered by parents and others who work with children with Attention Deficit Disorder and learning and behavior problems.

AFFECT—Moods, feelings, or emotions.

ALEXIA—Loss of the ability to read written or printed language.

ANOXIA—Reduced supply of oxygen for a long enough time to cause brain injury.

APHASIA (DYSPHASIA)—Loss or impairment of the ability to understand or formulate language; caused by neurological damage.

AUDIOGRAM—A graphic representation of the weakest sound a person can hear at several frequency levels.

AUDITORY CLOSURE—The ability to recognize a whole word or phrase from the presentation of a partial auditory stimulus.

AUDITORY RECEPTION—The ability to derive meaning from orally presented material.

AUDITORY SEQUENTIAL MEMORY—The ability to remember a sequence of auditory stimuli.

AVERSIVE STIMULUS—A stimulus that a subject will avoid if possible.

BEHAVIOR MODIFICATION—Changing behavior with a variety of techniques based on learning principles, such as conditioning and reinforcement.

CENTRAL NERVOUS SYSTEM (CNS)—That part of the nervous system to which sensory impulses are transmitted and from which motor impulses originate; the brain and spinal cord.

CEREBRAL DOMINANCE—An assumption that one cerebral hemisphere generally dominates the other in control of bodily movements. In most individuals the left side of the brain controls language and is considered the dominant hemisphere.

CHROMOSOME—One of the bodies in the nucleus of a cell that contains the genes.

CONGENITAL—Present in an individual at birth.

CRITERION REFERENCE TEST—A test designed to measure a child's development in terms of absolute levels of mastery, as opposed to the child's status relative to other children, as in a norm reference test.

DIAGNOSTIC PRESCRIPTIVE TEACHING—An educational strategy of delineating a child's strengths and weaknesses and then of designing a specific program for teaching on the basis of those findings.

DISINHIBITION—Lack of ability to refrain from response often resulting in hyperactivity and distractibility.

DISTRACTIBILITY—Being abnormally affected by external stimuli; easily diverted from a task.

DYSARTHRIA—Difficulty in the articulation of words due to involvement of the central nervous system.

DYSCALCULIA—Inability to perform mathematical computations.

DYSGRAPHIA—Inability to produce the motor movements required for handwriting.

DYSLEXIA—Impairment of the ability to read.

ELECTROENCEPHALOGRAPH—An instrument for recording electrical brain waves.

EMOTIONAL LABILITY—Frequent, and often sudden, changes in mood.

ENDOGENOUS—Originating from within; a term used to characterize a constitutional condition. (Compare with exogenous.)

EXOGENOUS—Developed or derived from external causes. (Compare with endogenous.)

EXPRESSIVE LANGUAGE DISABILITIES—Problems associated with the inability to express oneself verbally.

EXTERNAL LOCUS OF CONTROL—A personality characteristic in which the individual believes chance factors or people other than himself are responsible for personal successes and failures.

EXTINCTION—Reduction or elimination of behavior by removing all reinforcement.

FAMILIAL—Occurring in members of the same family, as a familial disease.

FIGURE-GROUND DISTURBANCE—The inability to discriminate a figure from its background.

GENE—Responsible for hereditary characteristics; arranged at specific locations in the chromosomes within each cell.

GENETICS—The study of heredity.

GENIUS—A word sometimes used to indicate a particular aptitude or capacity in any area; rare intellectual powers.

GIFTEDNESS—Refers to cognitive (intellectual) superiority, creativity, and motivation in combination and of sufficient magnitude to set the child apart from the vast majority of age-mates and make it possible for him to contribute something of particular value to society.

HYPERACTIVE—Excessive movement or motor restlessness.

HYPOACTIVE—Diminished motor function or activity.

HYPOGLYCEMIA—A condition characterized by abnormally low blood sugar.

IMPULSIVITY—The tendency to respond quickly without carefully considering the alternatives; responding without adequate reflection; seeming to act without thinking.

INTERNAL LOCUS OF CONTROL—A personality characteristic in which the individual believes he is responsible for his own successes and failures.

IQ (INTELLIGENCE QUOTIENT)—A measure of intellectual functioning; average IQ set at 100.

LATERALITY—Awareness of the two sides of the body and the ability to identify left and right; often used to mean preferential use of one side of the body.

LEAST RESTRICTIVE ALTERNATIVE—The philosophy of bringing individuals with disabilities as close to the normal school and social setting as possible.

MAINSTREAMING—An administrative procedure for keeping exceptional children in the normal classroom for the majority of the school day.

MEGAVITAMIN THERAPY—The use of large doses of vitamins to treat ADD, learning disabilities, and a number of mental disorders.

MINIMAL BRAIN DYSFUNCTION—A poorly defined syndrome often including hyperactivity, distractibility, perseveration, and disorders of perception, body image, laterality, and sometimes symbolization; not used in this book because of its ambiguity.

NEUROLOGY—A medical specialty dealing with the study and treatment of disorders of the nervous system.

NEUROPHYSIOLOGICAL—Pertaining to the physiology of the nervous system.

ORGANIC—Inherent, inborn; involving known neurological or structural abnormality.

PERCEPTION—Refers to an individual's ability to process stimuli meaningfully; the ability to organize and interpret sensory information.

PERCEPTUAL-MOTOR IMPAIRMENT—Problems coordinating a visual or auditory stimulus with a motor act.

PERSEVERATION—Persistent repetition of an activity or a behavior.

POSTNATAL—After birth.

PRENATAL—Occurring or existing before birth.

PROPRIOCEPTIVE—Pertaining to stimulations from the muscles and tendons which give information concerning the position and movement of the body and its members.

PSYCHOMETRICS—Refers to standardized psychological tests such as tests of intelligence, perception, and personality.

PSYCHOPATHOLOGY—The study of the causes and nature of mental disorders.

RECEPTIVE LANGUAGE DISABILITIES—Difficulties that derive from the inability to understand spoken language.

REINFORCEMENT—A procedure to strengthen a response by the administration of immediate rewards (positive reinforcement).

RESOURCE TEACHER—A teacher who typically provides services for the exceptional children and their teachers within one school, assesses the particular needs of such children, and sometimes teaches them individually or in small groups, using any special materials or methods that are needed; consults with regular teachers, advising on the instruction and management of the children in the classroom and demonstrating instructional techniques.

RETICULAR ACTIVATING SYSTEM—A network of neurons that passes through the brainstem. Associated with wakefulness, arousal, and sleep.

SPECIAL EDUCATION—Providing instruction and supportive services for children with special learning needs.

SPECIAL SELF-CONTAINED CLASS—Enrolls exceptional children with a particular diagnostic label; usually children within such a class need full-time instruction in this placement and are only integrated with their normal classmates for a few activities, if any.

STIMULUS—The physical, chemical, biological, and social events that act on the individual.

STIMULUS REDUCTION—A concept largely forwarded by Cruickshank; an approach to teaching distractible and hyperactive children that emphasizes reducing extraneous (nonrelevant to learning) material.

SYNDROME—A set of characteristics or symptoms which occur together. Attention Deficit Disorder is a syndrome.

Appendix

Rating Scales

These rating scales can be ordered from the addresses listed below:

Child Assessment Schedule (CAS) Diagnostic Interview. (Listed in Catalog of Selected Documents in Psychology, 11:56.) American Psychological Association, 1200 Seventeenth Street Northwest, Washington, D.C. 20036

The Behavior Problem Check List. Herbert C. Quay, Ph.D., The University of Miami, Coral Gables, Florida 33124

The Child Behavior Check List, Child Profile, Teacher's Report Form and Direct Observation Form. Dr. Thomas Achenbach, Department of Psychiatry, The University of Vermont, One South Prospect Street, Burlington, Vermont 05401

Personality Inventory for Children (PIC). Western Psychological Services, 12031 Wilshire Boulevard, Los Angeles, California 90025

Professional and Parent Organizations

Listed below are the names and addresses of societies, organizations, and agencies serving families and children with special needs. Many can supply additional information and material which you may find useful.

Council for Exceptional Children
1920 Association Drive
Reston, Virginia 22091

Family Service Association of America
44 East 23rd Street
New York, New York 10010

Foundation for Child Development
345 East 46th Street
New York, New York 10017

National Committee for Multi-handicapped Children
239 14th Street
Niagara Falls, New York 14303

National Information Center for the Handicapped
Box 1492
Washington, D.C. 20013

American Foundation on Learning Disabilities
P.O. Box 196
Convent Station, New Jersey 07961

Association for Children and Adults with Learning Disabilities (ACLD)
4156 Library Road
Pittsburgh, Pennsylvania 15234
(Affiliate organizations in all states)

Directory of Facilities and Services for the Learning Disabled
Academic Therapy Publications
20 Commercial Boulevard
Novato, California 94949

National Learning Disabilities Assistance Project
The NETWORK
Merrimac, Massachusetts 01860

Publication List
Oklahoma Association for Children with Learning Disabilities
3701 Northwest 62nd Street
Oklahoma City, Oklahoma 73112

American Association of Psychiatric Clinics for Children
250 West 57th Street
Room 1032
New York, New York 10019

National Association for Mental Health
10 Columbus Circle
New York, New York 10019

U.S. Office of Vocational Education
400 Maryland Avenue S.W.
Washington, D.C. 20202

Allergy Foundation of America
801 Second Avenue
New York, New York 10017

U.S. Office of Education
Bureau of Education for the Handicapped
400 Maryland Avenue S.W.
Washington, D.C. 20202

National Rehabilitation Association
1522 K Street N.W.
Washington, D.C. 20005

Foundation for Attentional Disorders
Box 339 Station "D"
Toronto, Ontario M6P 3J9
Canada

Commonly Used Reinforcers

This list may give you some ideas for reinforcers to use with your child, but keep in mind that what may be a reward for one child may be unimportant to another. You know your child best.

Edible

candy	soda pop	nuts
gum	cakes	sweet cereal
popcorn	pies	
raisins	ice cream	

Many parents are reluctant to use sweets or other edible treats as reinforcers. We agree that they should be used cautiously and in very small amounts. They are, however, powerful rewards, especially for young children in the early stages of a behavior change program.

Social

attention	telephone privilege
praise	hours out of house
approval	choice of meal
private areas	having friend visit
time alone with parent	bedtime choices
dinner out	TV privilege, such as choosing
access to special areas, such as	program
TV room, den, etc.	

Activity

gym time	hobbies
shop time	theater
library time	ballet
driving privileges	sports teams
movies	camping
concerts	travel
field trips	

Other

balloons	car parts
clothing items	motorcycle and bicycle parts
toys	telephone
sports-related items	accessories/equipment for room
records	(TV, posters, dolls)
music equipment	

Revised Terminology and Diagnostic Criteria

The forthcoming revision of the Diagnostic and Statistical Manual of the American Psychiatric Association (DSM III-R) will include another change in terminology for the syndrome we now call Attention Deficit Disorder. DSM III-R will use the term Attention Deficit Hyperactivity Disorder. This name change represents a continuing effort on the part of research workers and clinicians to find the best possible way to describe the syndrome. It is likely that subsequent revisions of the diagnostic manual will result in further changes in terminology. Nonetheless, the nature of the disorder, its defining characteristics, and its treatment remain, for the most part, the same.

Criteria for diagnosing Attention Deficit Hyperactivity Disorder are as follows.

A disturbance of at least six months during which at least eight of the following are present:

1. Often fidgets with hands or feet or squirms in seat
2. Has difficulty remaining seated when required to do so
3. Is easily distracted by extraneous stimuli
4. Has difficulty waiting turn in games or group situations
5. Often blurts out answers to questions before they have been completed
6. Has difficulty following through on instructions from others
7. Has difficulty sustaining attention in tasks or play activities
8. Often shifts from one uncompleted activity to another
9. Has difficulty playing quietly
10. Often talks excessively
11. Often interrupts or intrudes on others
12. Often does not seem to listen to what is being said to him or her
13. Often loses things necessary for tasks or activities at school or at home
14. Often engages in physically dangerous activities without considering the possible consequences

Attention Deficit Disorder

A Workshop
for Psychologists, Social Workers,
Counselors, and Parents
Presented by Educational Resources Center
and
Ronald J. Friedman, Ph.D.

Dr. Friedman, co-author of *Attention Deficit Disorder and Hyperactivity,* is available to present either a half-day or a full-day workshop in your area for professionals and/or parents. The program can be developed to fit the needs of your particular community.

For further information write:

Ronald J. Friedman, Ph.D.
19900 Ten Mile Road
St. Clair Shores, MI 48081
Phone: (313) 776-2949